AF305194

ASH KEATING
MUSEUM LANGMATT

ASH KEATING

MUSEUM LANGMATT

Markus Stegmann (Hrsg. / Ed.)

Museum Langmatt, Baden
Stiftung Langmatt
Sidney und Jenny Brown

Hatje Cantz

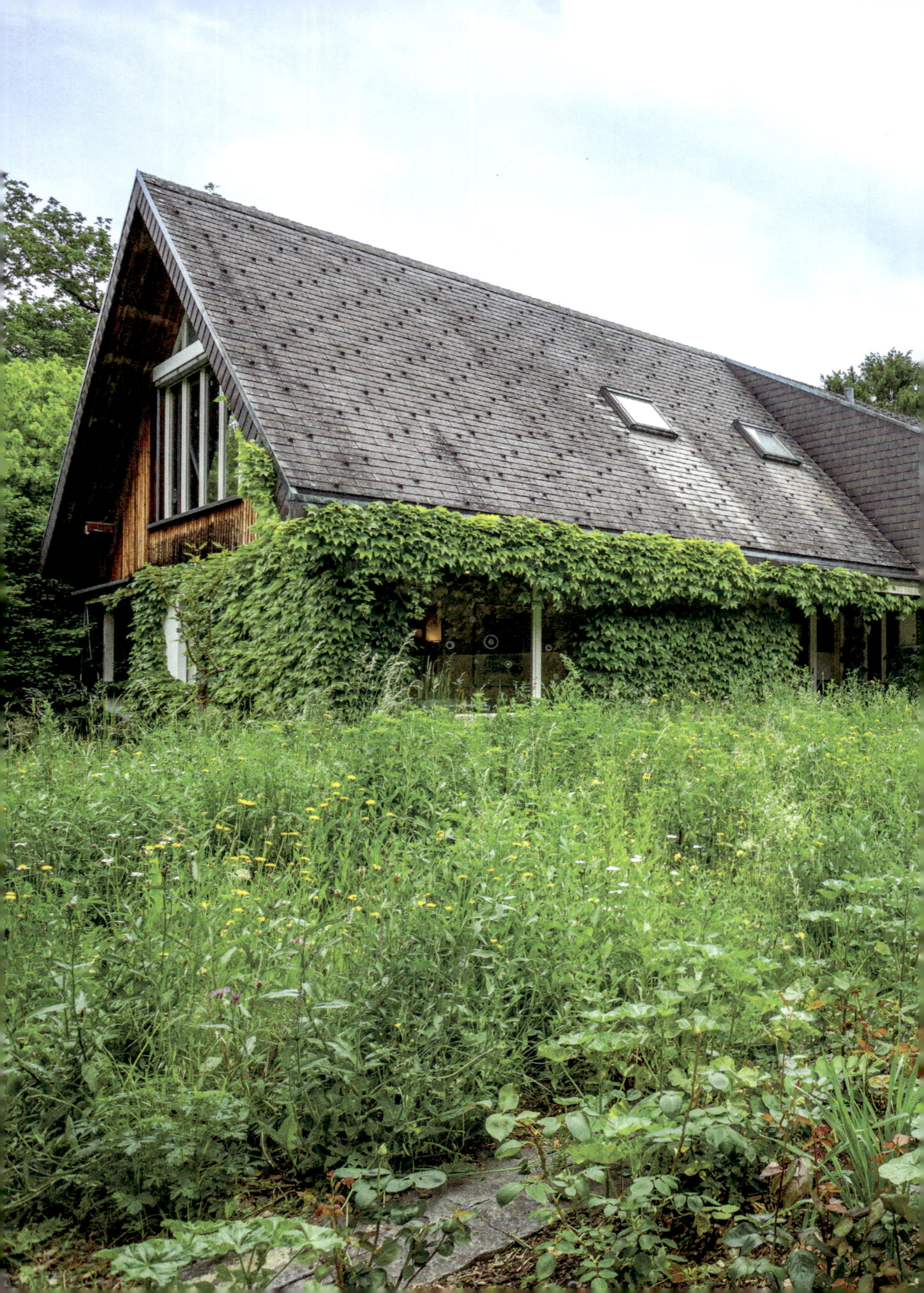

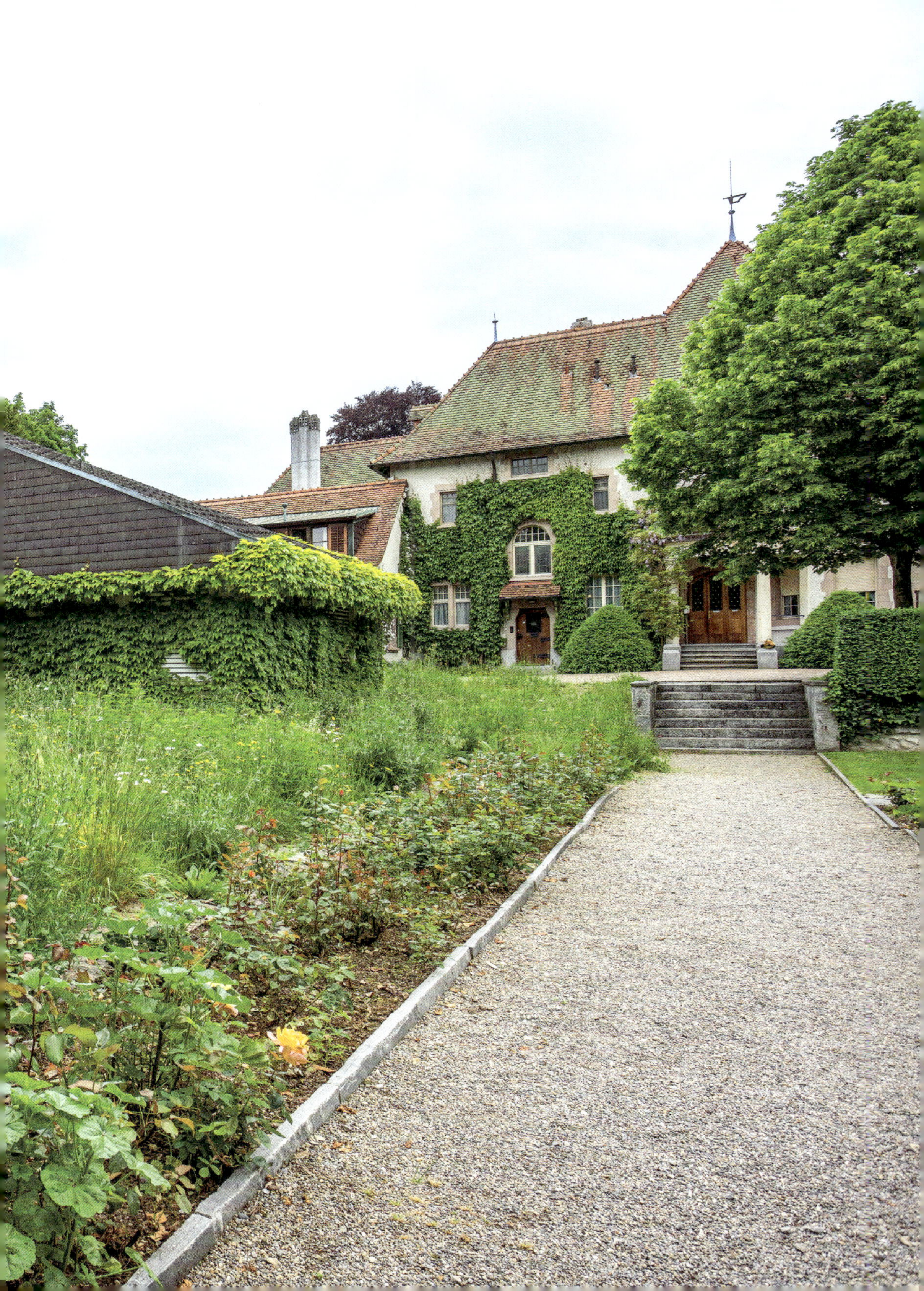

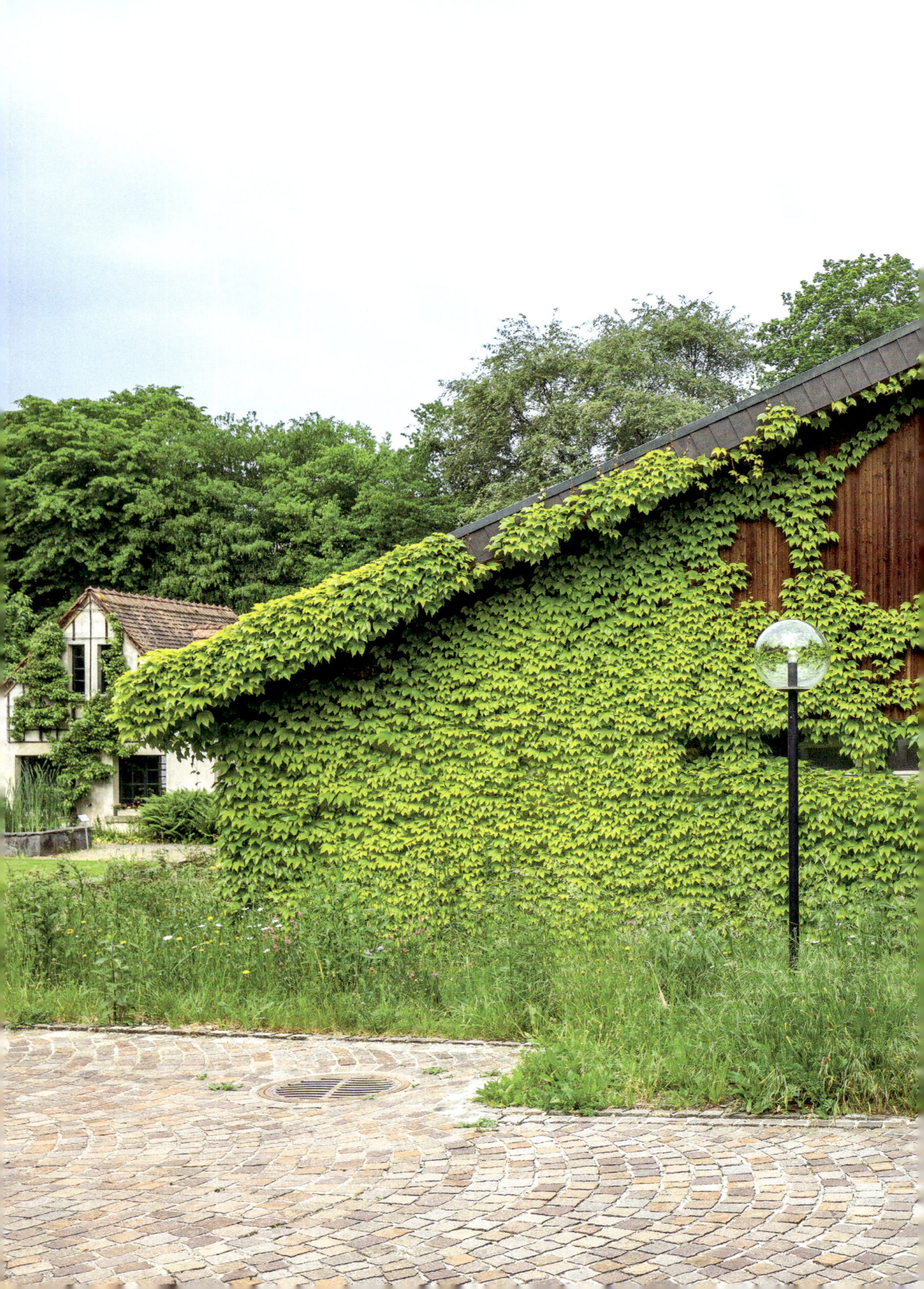

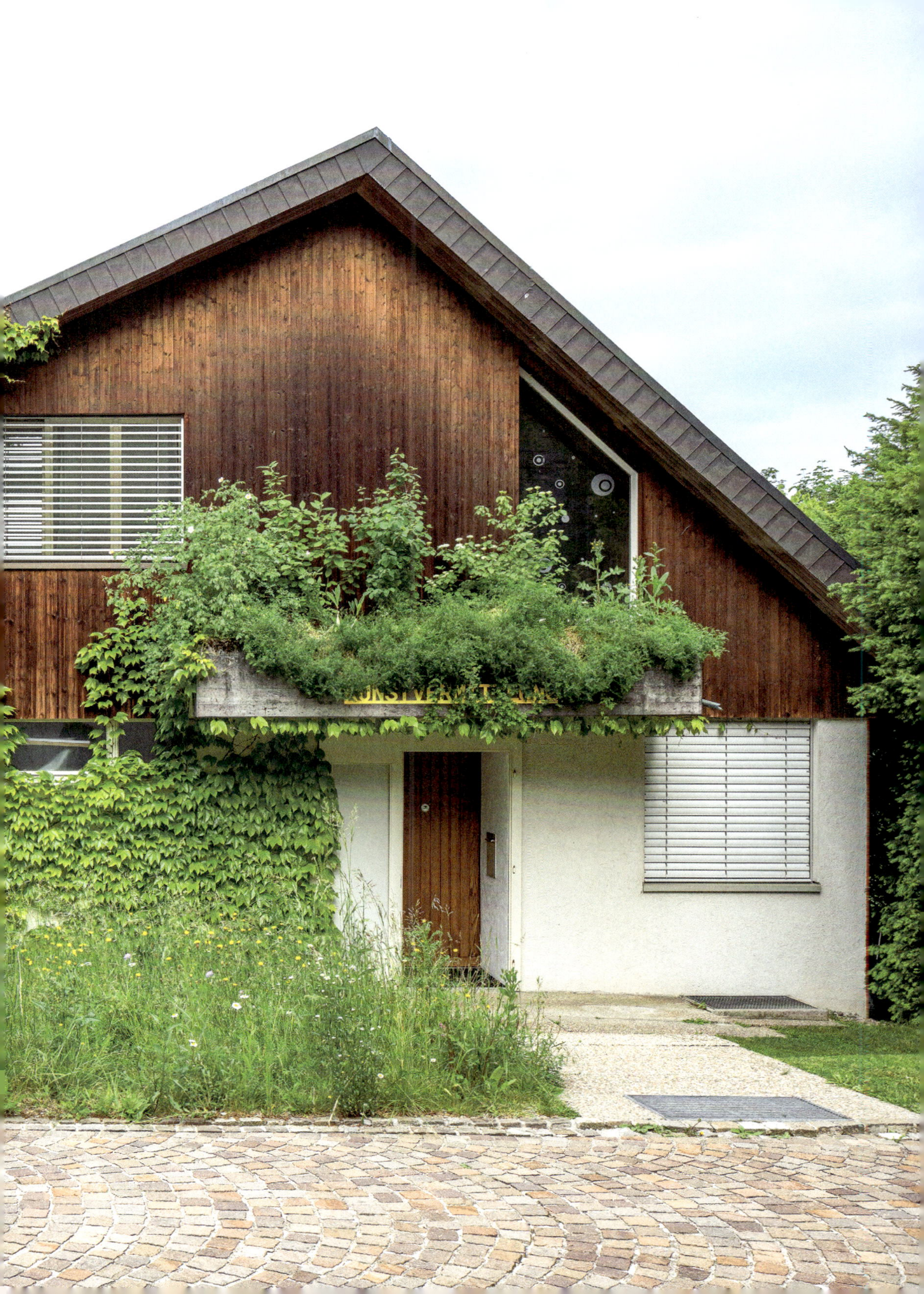
KUNSTVERMITTLUNG

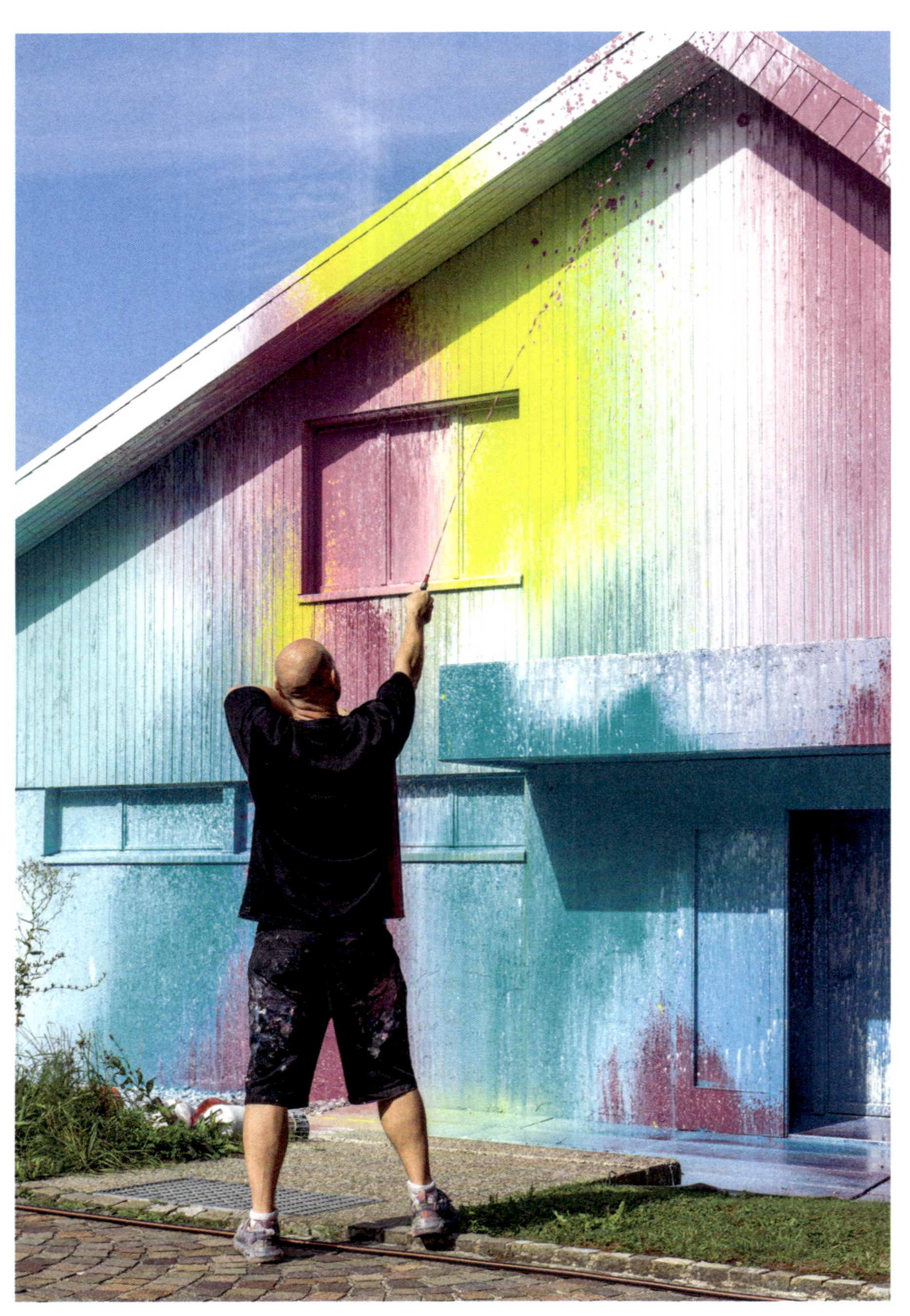

DANIELA MINNEBOO

EXPLOSIVE
FARBEN.
*HAUS GERMANN
RESPONSE*
VON ASH KEATING

EXPLOSIVE
COLOURS:
*HAUS GERMANN
RESPONSE*
BY ASH KEATING

The astonishing transformation of the Haus Germann from a grey, standard 1970s single-family home which has led a rather neglected existence in the shadow of the Brown family's art nouveau villa since it was built to a three-dimensional painting in the most brilliant colours was completed in just a few hours – after weeks of preparation. On 17 of August 2023, in a spectacular piece of action art, the Australian artist Ash Keating (*1980 in Melbourne) sprayed the building with fountains of paint out of fire extinguishers, transforming it into a sparkling crystal in the heart of the Langmatt park. Shortly before the demolition, in the final months of its existence, the house blooms – before its replacement by a glazed pavilion that is to be created during the complete renovation of the Museum from 2024–25. This artwork serves as a harbinger and symbol of the potential for renewal and the imminent transformation of the Langmatt. During the two-week preparation period for the painting process, the artist observed the position of the sun and found that in the morning it reaches Haus Germann at about half past nine. The long shadow of the historic villa, located east of Haus Germann, has vanished by that time. In the late afternoon, when the sun is beginning to set, the western side of the house is lit up. This is why he divided the painting time into two stages: a one-and-a-half-hour session in the morning, and a further session in the afternoon. The public were invited to watch the artist at work, and they accepted this invitation in large numbers. On the day before the opening of the Badenfahrt fair, a total of almost 350 people witnessed the spectacle.

Die erstaunliche Transformation des Haus Germann von einem grauen Standard-Einfamilienhaus von 1970, das zeitlebens ein stiefmütterliches Dasein im Schatten der Jugendstil-Villa von Familie Brown fristete, zu einem dreidimensionalen Gemälde in den schillerndsten Farben vollzog sich – nach wochenlangen Vorbereitungen – innerhalb weniger Stunden. In einer spektakulären Aktion am 17. August 2023 hat der australische Künstler Ash Keating (*1980 in Melbourne/Australien) das Haus mit Farbfontänen, die aus Feuerlöschern geschossen kamen, besprayt und in einen funkelnden Kristall inmitten des Langmatt-Parks verwandelt. Kurz vor dem Abriss, in den letzten Monaten seiner Existenz, blüht das Haus auf, bevor es einem gläsernen Pavillon weicht, der im Rahmen der Gesamtsanierung des Museums 2024/25 entstehen wird. Das Kunstwerk wird zum Vorboten und Symbol für das Erneuerungspotenzial und die bevorstehende Transformation der Langmatt.
Während der zweiwöchigen Vorbereitungszeit der Bemalung hat der Künstler den Sonnenstand beobachtet und festgestellt, dass die morgendliche Sonne das Haus Germann um etwa halb zehn Uhr erreicht. Die langen Schatten der historischen Villa, östlich von Haus Germann gelegen, haben sich dann verflüchtigt. Am späteren Nachmittag, wenn die Sonne bereits wieder zum Untergang ansetzt, liegt die westliche Seite des Hauses im Licht. Die Bemalung hat er deswegen in zwei Etappen aufgeteilt: je eine eineinhalb-stündige Session am Vor- und eine am Nachmittag. Das Publikum war eingeladen, dem Künstler bei der Arbeit zuzusehen, und es ist dieser Einladung in grosser Zahl gefolgt. Insgesamt haben knapp 350 Personen das Spektakel am Tag vor der Eröffnung der Badenfahrt miterlebt.

Der Titel des Kunstwerks, *Haus Germann Response* (engl. «response» zu Deutsch: «Antwort» oder «Reaktion»), spielt darauf an, dass sich Ash Keating bei der Farbwahl von der umliegenden Natur hat inspirieren lassen. Die violetten Blumen, die im nahen Sumpfbeet wachsen, die rosaroten, gelben und orangen Rosen im Beet entlang des Kieswegs, aber auch das Grün der Wiesen und Bäume rund um das Haus finden sich in seiner Auswahl. Obwohl gerade Grün eine Farbe ist, die der Künstler sonst nicht verwendet. Weitere Inspiration boten ihm Werke aus der Sammlung des Museums, insbesondere die Landschaften von Pierre-Auguste Renoir (1841–1919). Das saftige, helle, fast gelbe Grün in Gemälden wie *Das Boot* (um 1878) oder *Auf der Insel Chatou* (um 1879) interessierte ihn dabei besonders. Der üppige Blätterwald, der die Szenerie in *Das Boot* umgibt, erweckt wegen des saftigen Grüns den Eindruck, man befinde sich in einem Dschungel. Dies ist unter anderem der «Nass in Nass»-Technik von Renoir geschuldet, die in ähnlicher Form auch von Ash Keating angewendet wurde.

Aus einem Grundstock an Farben, die wir von verschiedenen Sponsoren erhalten haben, hat Ash Keating seine Farbpalette zusammengemischt. Auch wenn noch ein kleiner Teil dazugekauft werden musste, konnten wir für das Projekt hauptsächlich mit Farbresten arbeiten, die sonst entsorgt worden wären. Somit hat nicht nur das Haus Germann ein zweites Leben erhalten, sondern auch die Farben, mit denen es bemalt ist.

Die Bemalungen begannen damit, dass Ash Keating die vorbereiteten Feuerlöscher um den jeweils zu bemalenden Hausteil herum aufstellte und so eine erste Auslegeordnung für die Farbgebung kreierte. Die mit einem Luftkompressor unter Druck gesetzten Feuerlöscher kamen aber nicht gleich zum Einsatz, sondern zunächst ein Wasserschlauch, mit dem er die Aussenhülle

The title of the artwork, *Haus Germann Response*, alludes to the fact that Keating was inspired by the surrounding natural environment when choosing the colours. His chosen colours echo the violet flowers that grow in the nearby swamp bed, the pink, yellow and orange roses in the bed along the gravel path, but also the green of the meadows and trees around the house – although green in particular is a colour that the artist does not normally use. He was additionally inspired by artworks from the museum's collection – in particular, the landscapes of Pierre-Auguste Renoir (1841–1919). Keating was particularly interested in the juicy, bright greens – almost yellow-green – seen in paintings such as *The Boat* (circa 1878) or *On the Island of Chatou* (circa 1879). The lush leafy forest of the surrounding scenery in *The Boat* and the lush greenery in general gives the impression that the setting is a jungle. This is due, among other things, to Renoir's 'wet on wet' technique, which was also used by Keating in a similar form.

Keating mixed his colour palette from a stock of paints we received from various sponsors. Although a small amount had to be purchased, we were able to realise the project primarily using paint residues that would otherwise have been disposed of. Thus, not only the Haus Germann but also the paints with which the building was painted have been given a second lease on life.

The paintings began with Ash Keating placing the prepared fire extinguishers around the part of the house to be painted, thus creating an initial layout for the colour scheme. The fire extinguishers pressurized with an air compressor, however, were not used immediately – initially, a water hose was used to extensively wet the outer shell.

After the first fountains of colour had been poured over the house, he added water again, brightening the bright colours and making them appear more brilliant while at the same time creating fascinating, almost transcendent colour gradients. This technique is reminiscent of Renoir's 'wet-on-wet' technique, which involved applying the oil paint in a single stage instead of letting the individual layers dry as is usual. Keating's fascination with fluid colours may have its origins in an experience from his early adolescence, when he flew with his grandmother in a small plane over the vast Australian landscape. This experience of the landscape sweeping by had a deep impact on him: in an interview in this catalogue (p. 62) he says that it provided the initial spark for his desire to become an artist. Then as now, his art has its origins in his observation of nature, with his artworks serving as 'responses' – i.e. reactions to it. Despite its unbelievable brightness and luminosity, the painting of Haus Germann also blends organically into the park and its wider surroundings.

The eastern part of the house is decorated in perceptibly slightly lighter colours than those of the western part: the crisp morning sun seems to have inspired Keating to create bright, fresh colours, while during the afternoon session he used bolder and slightly darker tones. He reacted not only to the colours of the flowers, but also, in the spirit of the Impressionists, to the movements of light.

ausgiebig nässte. Auch nachdem sich die ersten Farbfontänen über das Haus ergossen, fügte er immer wieder Wasser hinzu, was die bunten Farben einerseits aufhellte und brillanter erscheinen liess, und gleichzeitig faszinierende, fast transzendente Farbverläufe schuf. Diese Technik erinnert an das «Nass in Nass» von Renoir, der die Ölfarbe in einem Maldurchgang auftrug, statt wie üblich die einzelnen Schichten trocknen zu lassen. Die Faszination Ash Keatings für fliessende Farben mag ihren Ursprung in einer Erfahrung haben, die er als Kind und Jugendlicher gemacht hat. Damals flog er mit seiner Grossmutter in einem kleinen Flugzeug über die Weiten der australischen Natur. Dieses Erlebnis der vorbeiziehenden Landschaft hat ihn tief geprägt, im Interview (S. 62) sagt er, es sei die Initialzündung gewesen für seinen Wunsch, Künstler zu werden. Damals wie heute hat seine Kunst ihren Ursprung in der Naturbeobachtung, und seine Werke sind «Responses», also Reaktionen darauf. Trotz der unglaublichen Buntfarbigkeit und Leuchtkraft fügt sich auch die Bemalung von Haus Germann organisch in den Park und die weitere Umgebung ein.

Es fällt auf, dass der östliche Teil des Hauses in etwas helleren Farben gehalten ist als der westliche. Die Morgensonne schien Ash Keating zu hellen, frischen Farben inspiriert zu haben, während bei der nachmittäglichen Session auch kräftigere und etwas dunklere Töne zum Einsatz kamen. Er reagierte also nicht nur auf die Farben der Blumen,

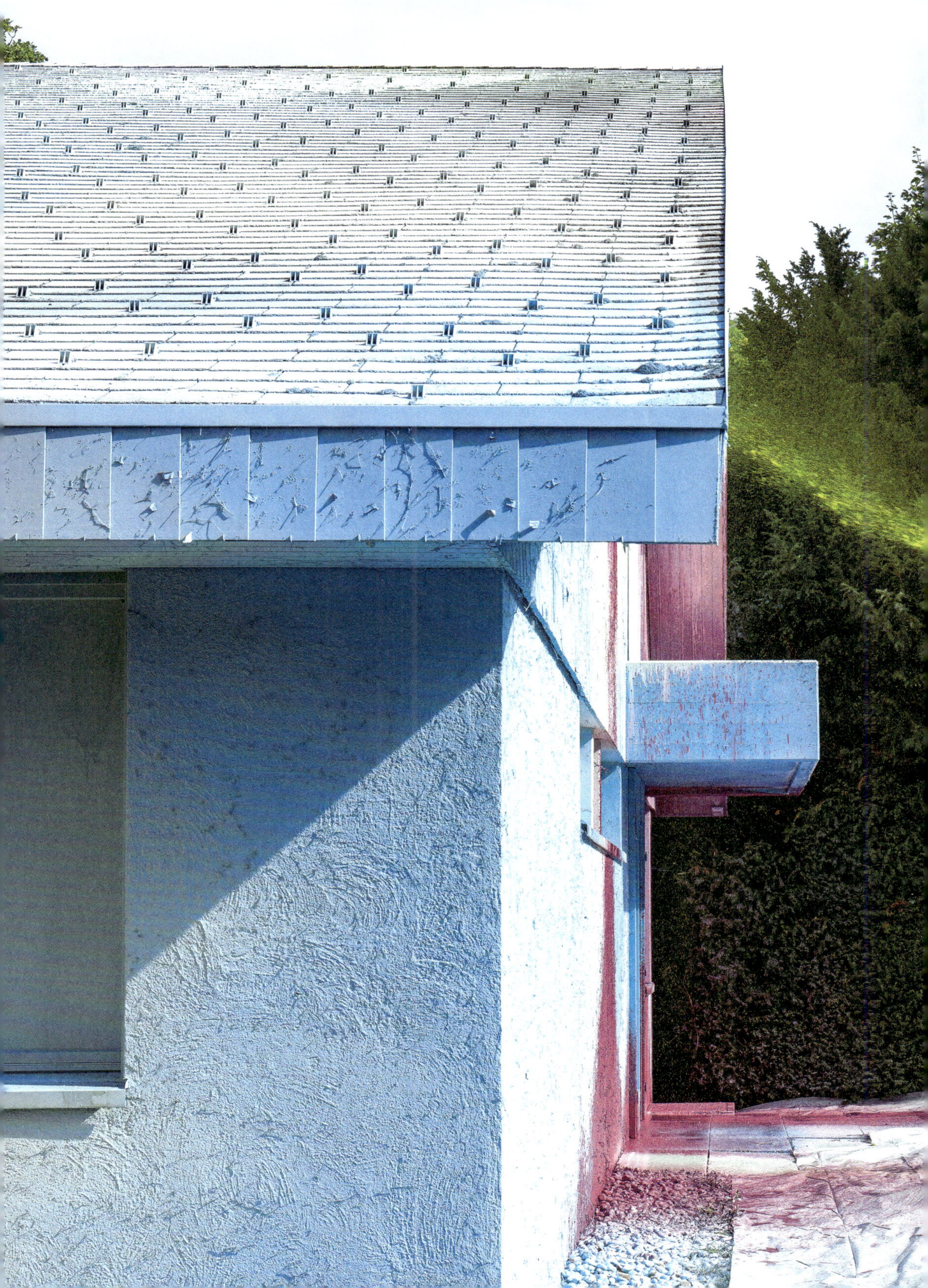

The spray radius of most of the fire extinguishers was relatively narrow, which meant that the paints were applied next to and on top of each other in lanes. The elongated stripes in shades of pink, magenta, orange, green and yellow are reminiscent of a rainbow or even of sweets. As the fire extinguishers emptied, the drops became larger due to the decreasing pressure. On the west façade –and especially around the former seating area – this led to larger patches of paint.

No other aids were used for the painting action, except for a grey membrane that protected the surrounding meadow from paint splashes. The fire extinguishers had a range of over eight meters, allowing Keating to catapult the paint over the entire roof all the way to the gable without having to climb onto a lifting platform or scaffolding. What looks easy at first glance was apparently a feat of strength for the artist, as the fire extinguishers were made of solid metal with a capacity of up to nine litres and had a considerable weight. The audience sat behind a generously-sized barrier, which ensured that they were not hit by the fountains of paint.

The technique of pouring paint into fire extinguishers and then pressuring them dates back to Keating's early artistic beginnings, a phase during which he secretly and illegally engaged in artistic activities on the streets of Melbourne at night. The fire extinguishers enabled him to quickly paint large areas – entire houses or huge walls. The large, expansive gesture of this technique, the bright, explosive colours, the interest in architecture and the making of art in the open air – qualities that

sondern, ganz im Sinne der Impressionisten, auch auf die Bewegungen des Lichts. Der Sprühradius der meisten Feuerlöscher war relativ eng, so dass sich die Farben in Bahnen neben- und aufeinander legten. Die länglichen Streifen in Pink-, Magenta-, Orange-, Grün- und Gelbtönen erinnern an einen Regenbogen oder auch an Süssigkeiten. Sobald sich die Feuerlöscher leerten, wurden die Tropfen wegen des nachlassenden Drucks grösser. Auf der Westfassade und insbesondere im Bereich des ehemaligen Sitzplatzes finden sich daher grössere Farbflecken.

Weitere Hilfsmittel waren für die Bemalungsaktionen nicht im Einsatz, bis auf eine graue Folie, die die umliegende Wiese vor Farbspritzern schütze. Mit über acht Metern Reichweite konnte Ash Keating die Farbe mit den Feuerlöschern über das ganze Dach bis zum Giebel katapultieren, ohne dass er auf eine Hebebühne oder ein Gerüst steigen musste. Was auf den ersten Blick leicht aussah, schien für den Künstler aber auch ein Kraftakt gewesen zu sein, hatten die Feuerlöscher aus massivem Metall mit bis zu 9 Litern Fassungsvermögen doch ein beträchtliches Gewicht. Das Publikum sass hinter einer grosszügig bemessenen Absperrung, um nicht von den Farbfontänen getroffen zu werden.

Die Technik, Farbe in Feuerlöscher zu füllen und sie anschliessend unter Druck zu setzen, stammt aus seinen künstlerischen Anfängen, in denen er sich nachts heimlich und illegal auf den Strassen Melbournes künstlerisch betätigte. Die Feuerlöscher ermöglichten ihm, schnell grosse Flächen, ganze Häuser oder riesige Wände zu bemalen. Diese grosse, ausladende Geste, die leuchtenden, explosiven Farben, die Beschäftigung mit Architektur und die Arbeit im Freien sind bis heute Kern seiner künstlerischen Arbeit und haben ihren Ursprung in der Street Art. Als weiteren Einfluss für seine Arbeit nennt Ash Keating das Künstlerpaar Christo (1935–2020) und Jeanne-Claude (1935–2009), die mit spektakulären Verhüllungsaktionen international grosse Bekanntheit erlangten. Tatsächlich wirkte das Haus Germann bereits nach der Grundierung seltsam verwandelt, als wäre an seiner statt ein überdimensionales Modellhaus aufgetaucht. Der Effekt war durchaus vergleichbar mit dem der mit Stoffbahnen verhüllten Gebäude, Brücken und Strände von Christo und Jeanne-Claude. Deren künstlerische Maxime, keine Stipendien oder Aufträge anzunehmen, sondern ihre mehrere hunderttausend Franken teuren Projekte ausschliesslich aus dem Verkauf vorgängig angefertigter Skizzen zu finanzieren, wahrte ihre kreative Unabhängigkeit. Auch sie setzten ihre Aktionen zu Beginn ihrer Karriere manchmal illegal um, wenn sie keine Bewilligung für die Projekte erhielten. Die Kunst raus aus den Museen, in die Strassen und zu den Menschen zu bringen, niederschwellig und manchmal auch widerständig, ist ein Kernthema der Street Art und zeichnet auch diese beiden künstlerischen Positionen aus. Die Transformation und Verwandlung von bekannten, kaum mehr wahrgenommenen Objekten im öffentlichen Raum schärft die Wahrnehmung, verblüfft und begeistert zugleich.

have their origins in street art – are still at the core of his artistic work today. As an additional influence on his work, Keating cites the artist couple Christo (1935–2020) and Jeanne-Claude (1935–2009), who gained international fame with their spectacular wrapping art events. In fact, the Germann House appeared strangely transformed after the primer was applied, as if an oversized model house had appeared in its place. The effect was quite reminiscent of Christo and Jeanne-Claude's covering of buildings, bridges and beaches with panels of fabric. Their creative independence was preserved by their artistic maxim of not accepting grants or commissions, but instead financing their projects – which cost thousands of euros – exclusively from the sale of pre-made sketches. At the outset of their careers, they, too, sometimes carried out their actions illegally if they did not receive a permit for the projects. Bringing art out of the museums and into the streets and to the people, in a low-threshold and sometimes even guerrilla way, is a core tenet of street art, and also distinguishes these two artistic positions. The transformation and alteration of well-known, hardly-noticed objects in public spaces sharpens our perception, amazes and inspires at the same time.

The undercoat primer applied in advance played an important role in the effect of *Haus Germann Response*. The white paint had to be sprayed on in several layers using a special device over the course of the previous week, especially in the area of the wood panelling, which 'swallowed' paint considerably. Over the first white and light-green layers, Keating applied a number of cloudy blue areas. If you look at the fully painted house from a slightly greater distance, the effect of the white-blue primer becomes clearer. The surrounding greenery appears darker, and the Haus Germann, with its brightly coloured paint, stands out all the more brightly and radiantly. In his introductory speech, Markus Stegmann noted this effect and compared the artwork to an iceberg that had somehow become stranded in Baden. The impression of coldness that emanates from it connects with another work by Ash Keating in the Langmatt park. The artist has made an intensive study of Claude Monet's *Ice Floes at Twilight* (1893) from the Langmatt collection and displayed his interpretation of the painting on huge billboards in the museum's park.

Eine wichtige Rolle für die Wirkung von *Haus Germann Response* spielt die vorgängig angebrachte Grundierung. In mehreren Schichten und mit einem Spezialgerät musste die weisse Farbe in der Vorwoche aufgesprüht werden, insbesondere im Bereich der Holzverkleidung, die erheblich Farbe «schluckte». Über die ersten weissen und hellgrünen Lagen setzte Ash Keating einige wolkige blaue Flächen. Betrachtet man das fertig bemalte Haus aus etwas grösserer Distanz, tritt die Wirkung der weiss-blauen Grundierung deutlicher zutage. Das umliegende Grün verdunkelt sich, und das Haus Germann mit seiner buntfarbigen Bemalung tritt umso leuchtender und strahlender hervor. In der Einführungsrede hat Markus Stegmann auf diesen Effekt hingewiesen und das Kunstwerk mit einem Eisberg verglichen, der scheinbar in Baden gestrandet ist. Die vermeintliche Kälte, die von ihm ausgeht, kann mit einem weiteren Werk von Ash Keating im Park der Langmatt in Verbindung gebracht werden. Der Künstler hat sich intensiv mit Claude Monets *Eisschollen im Dämmerlicht* (1893) aus der Sammlung der Langmatt auseinandergesetzt und präsentiert seine Interpretation des Gemäldes auf riesigen Billboards im Park des Museums.

Das Haus Germann wird, wie eingangs erwähnt, im Rahmen der Gesamtsanierung im Frühjahr 2024 abgerissen. Es weicht einem multifunktionalen, gläsernen Pavillon, der für verschiedene Nutzungen zur Verfügung steht, zum Beispiel als Schlechtwettervariante für Gruppenanlässe. Das Haus wurde 1970 von zwei Söhnen der Familie, John und Harry Brown, für Paul Germann erbaut, der das Anwesen als Verwalter betreute. Nach dem Tod von Mutter Jenny Brown 1968 zog John Brown mit seiner Frau Andrée Marthe 1972 in die Langmatt. Als enger Vertrauter des letzten Erbens John Brown war Paul Germann massgeblich daran beteiligt, dass er die Langmatt nach seinem Tod der Stadt Baden vermachte und die Villa Langmatt ein öffentliches Museum wurde. Paul Germann hat bis kurz vor seinem Tod 2018 im Verwalterhaus gelebt, seitdem wird es vom Museum für die Kunstvermittlung, für Sitzungen, als Lagerraum und für andere Zwecke zwischengenutzt. Paul Germann selbst war, so heisst es, kein grosser Fan der Architektur des Hauses. Obwohl John Brown das Fertighaus speziell für die Bedürfnisse der Familie ausstatten liess, hat Paul Germann gelegentlich bemerkt, ihm wäre ein Haus «in französischem Stil» lieber gewesen.

Ash Keating hat dem Haus in den letzten Monaten seiner Existenz noch einmal Leben eingehaucht und es auf unvergleichliche Weise zum Strahlen gebracht. Das Werk wird mit dem Haus zusammen verschwinden und nur noch in Fotografien und Videos weiterleben. An einem Ort der Kontinuität, so Ash Keating, stellt diese zeitliche Limitierung einen wichtigen Kontrast dar und beweist gleichzeitig, dass auch ein historisches Ensemble wie die Langmatt sich verwandeln und erneuern kann.

As mentioned at the beginning, Haus Germann will be demolished in the spring of 2024 as part of the museum's complete renovation, to make way for a multifunctional, glass pavilion to be used, for example, as a venue for group events during bad weather. The house was built in 1970 by two sons of the family, John and Harry Brown, for Paul Germann, who looked after the property as caretaker. In 1972, after the death of his mother Jenny Brown in 1968, John Brown and his wife Andrée Marthe moved into the Langmatt. As a close confidant of John Brown, the last heir, Paul Germann was instrumental in Brown's decision to bequeath the Langmatt to the city of Baden after his death and for the Villa Langmatt to become a public museum. Paul Germann lived in the administrator's house until shortly before his death in 2018. Since then, it has been used by the museum for art education, for holding meetings, for storage and other purposes. It is said that Paul Germann himself was not much of a fan of the architecture of the house. Although John Brown had the prefabricated house set up especially for the needs of the family, Paul Germann sometimes remarked that he would have preferred a house 'in the French style'.

Ash Keating has breathed life into the house once more in the last months of its existence, making it incomparably radiant. This artwork will disappear along with the house, living on only in photographs and videos. In a place that represents continuity, according to Ash Keating, this temporally limited existence represents an important contrast, and, at the same time, proves that even a historical ensemble like the Langmatt can be transformed and renewed.

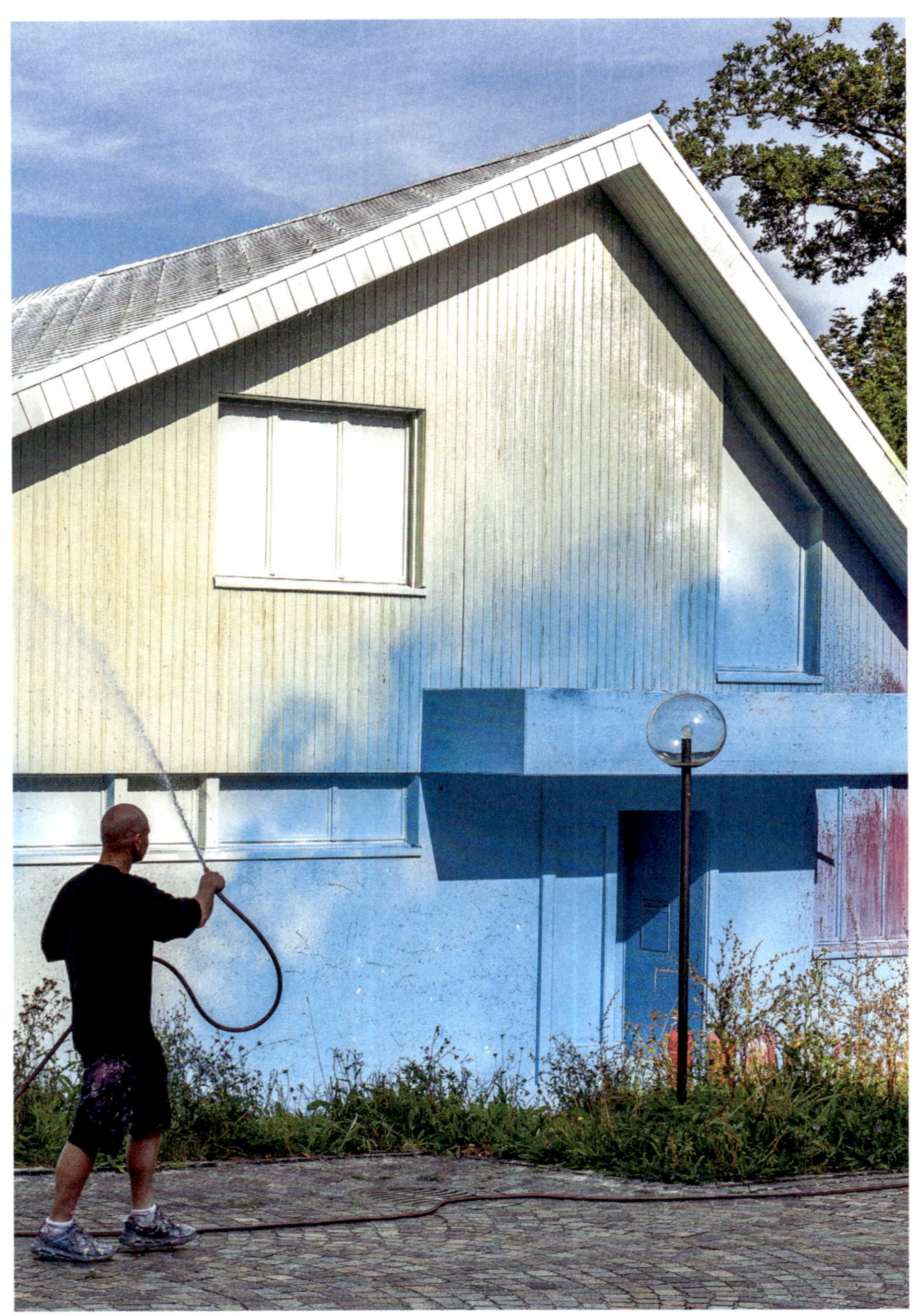

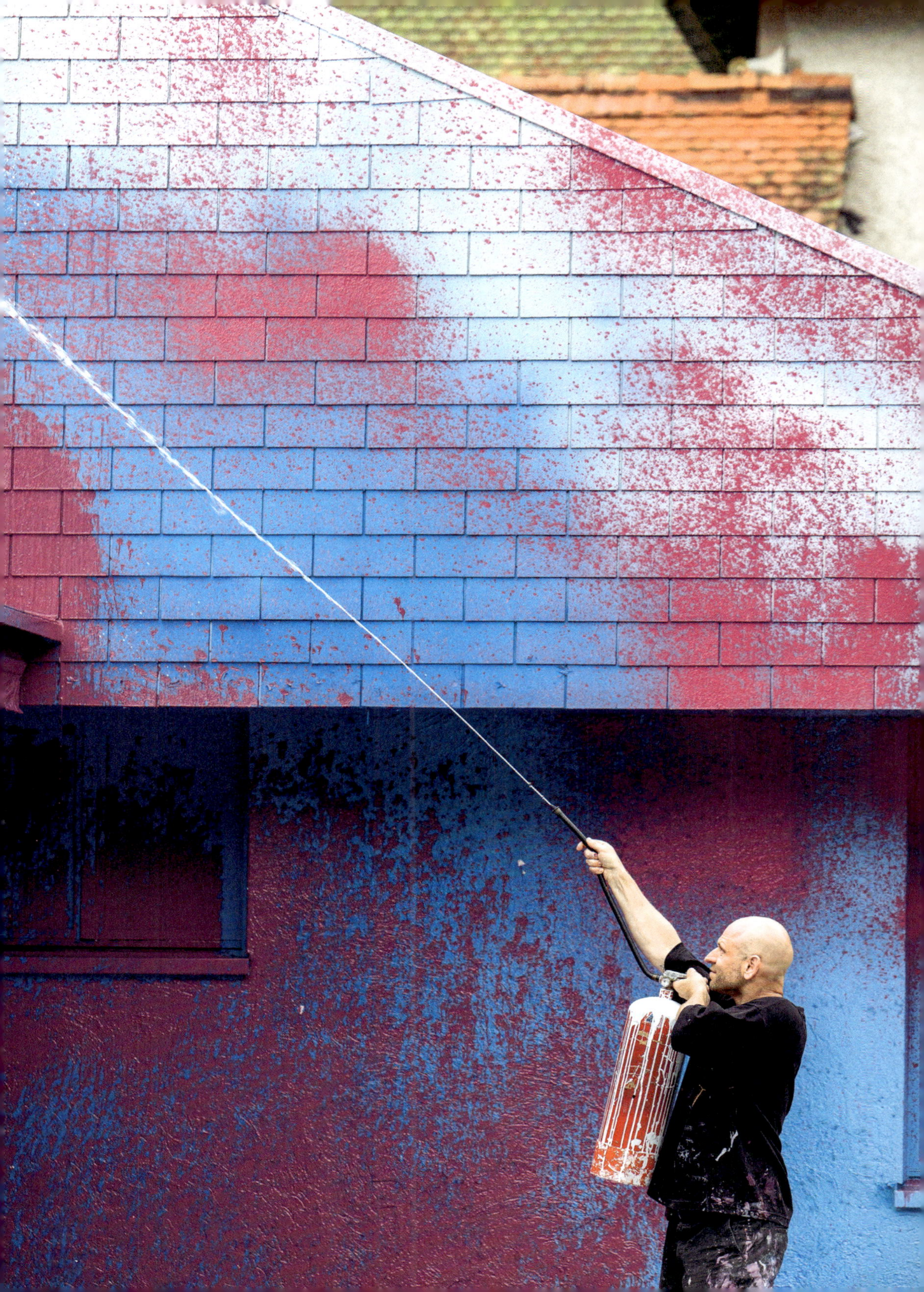

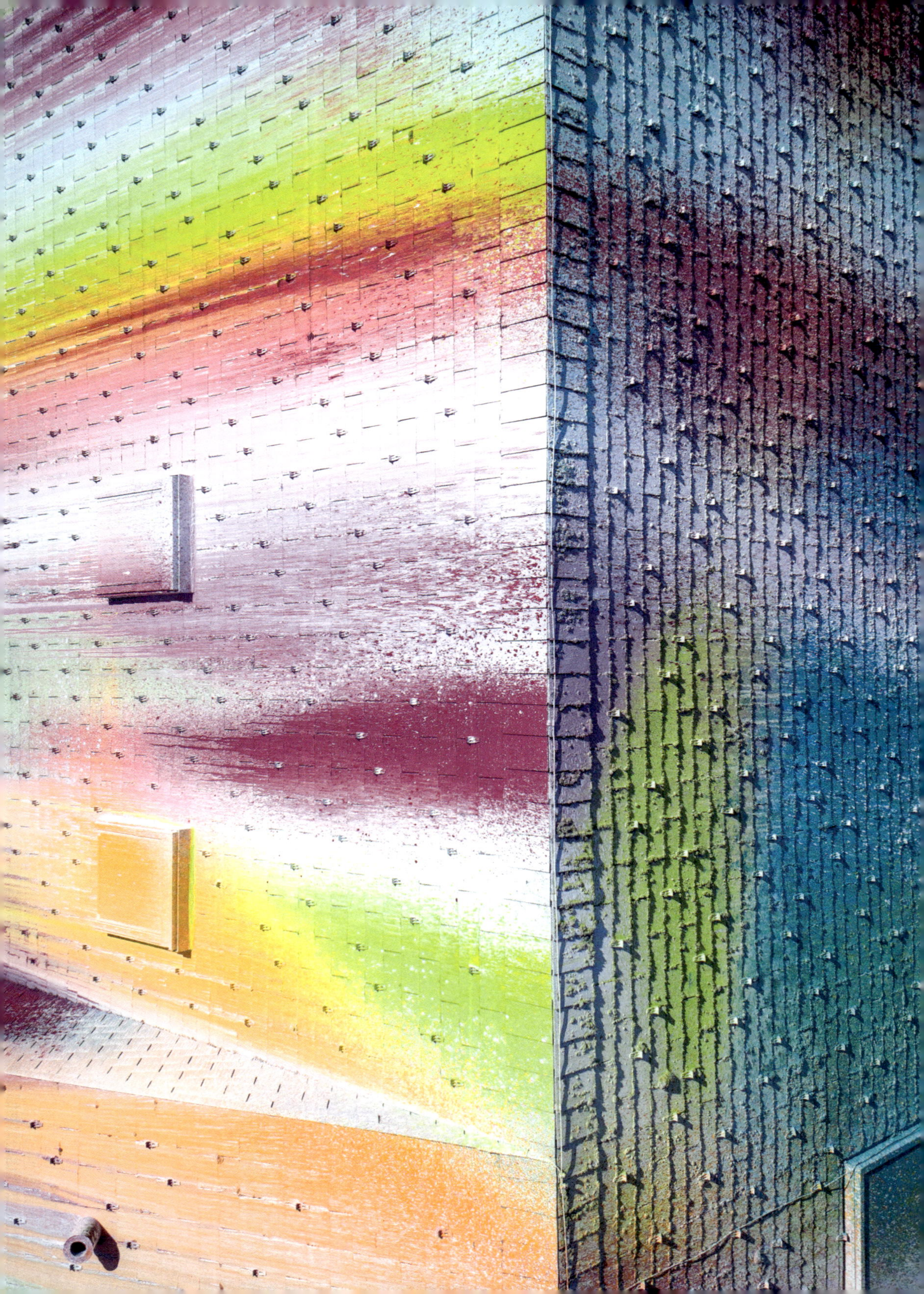

Haus Germann Response, 2023
13,8 × 14,9 × 6,8 m
Acryl- und Silikonharzfarbe /
Acrylic and silicon resin paint

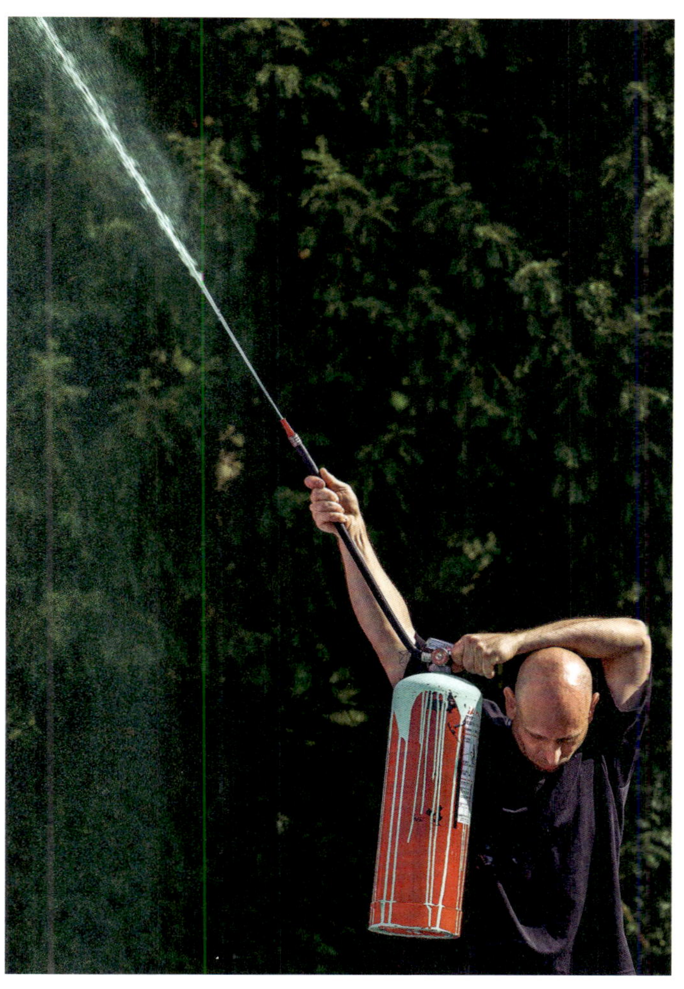

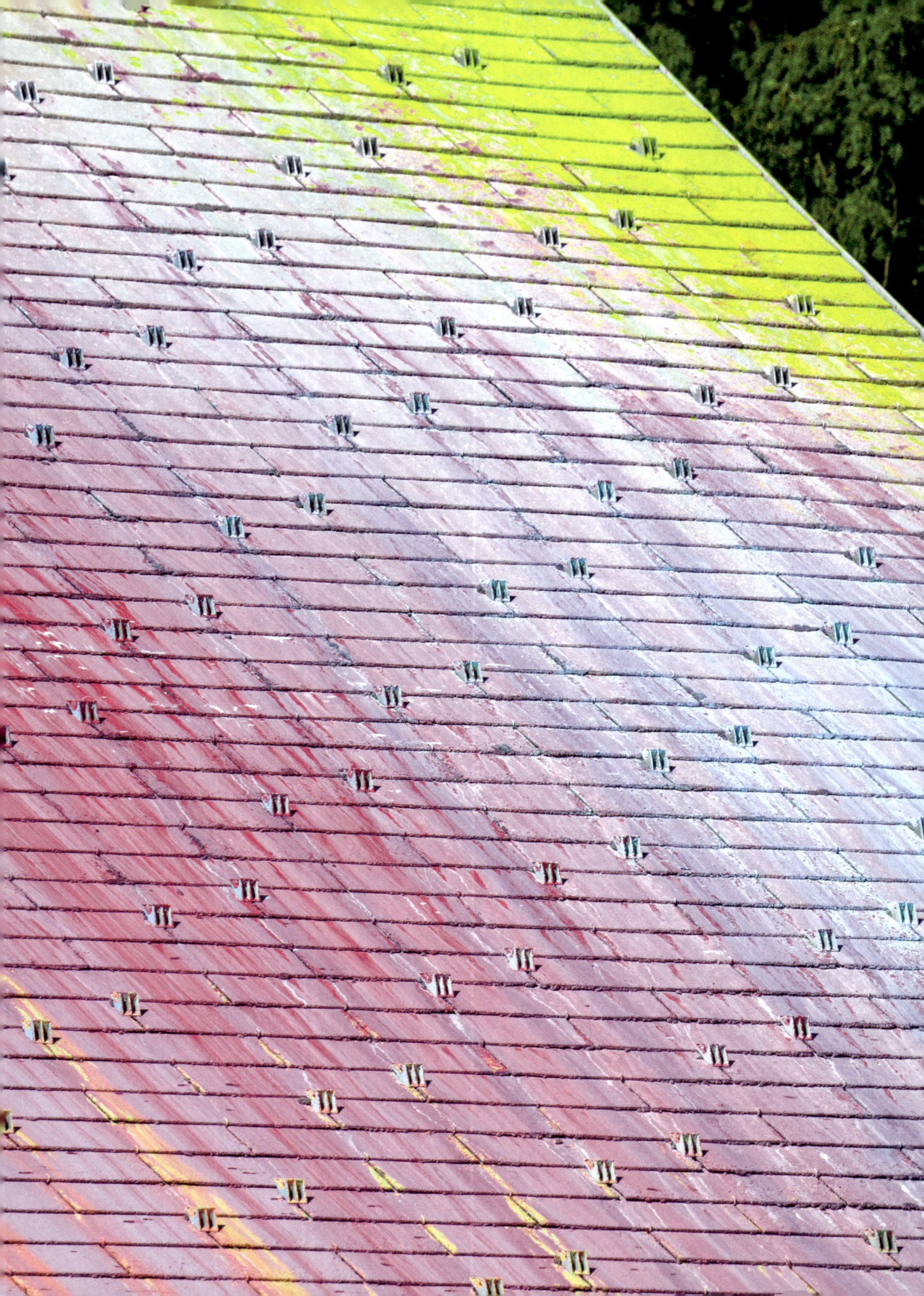

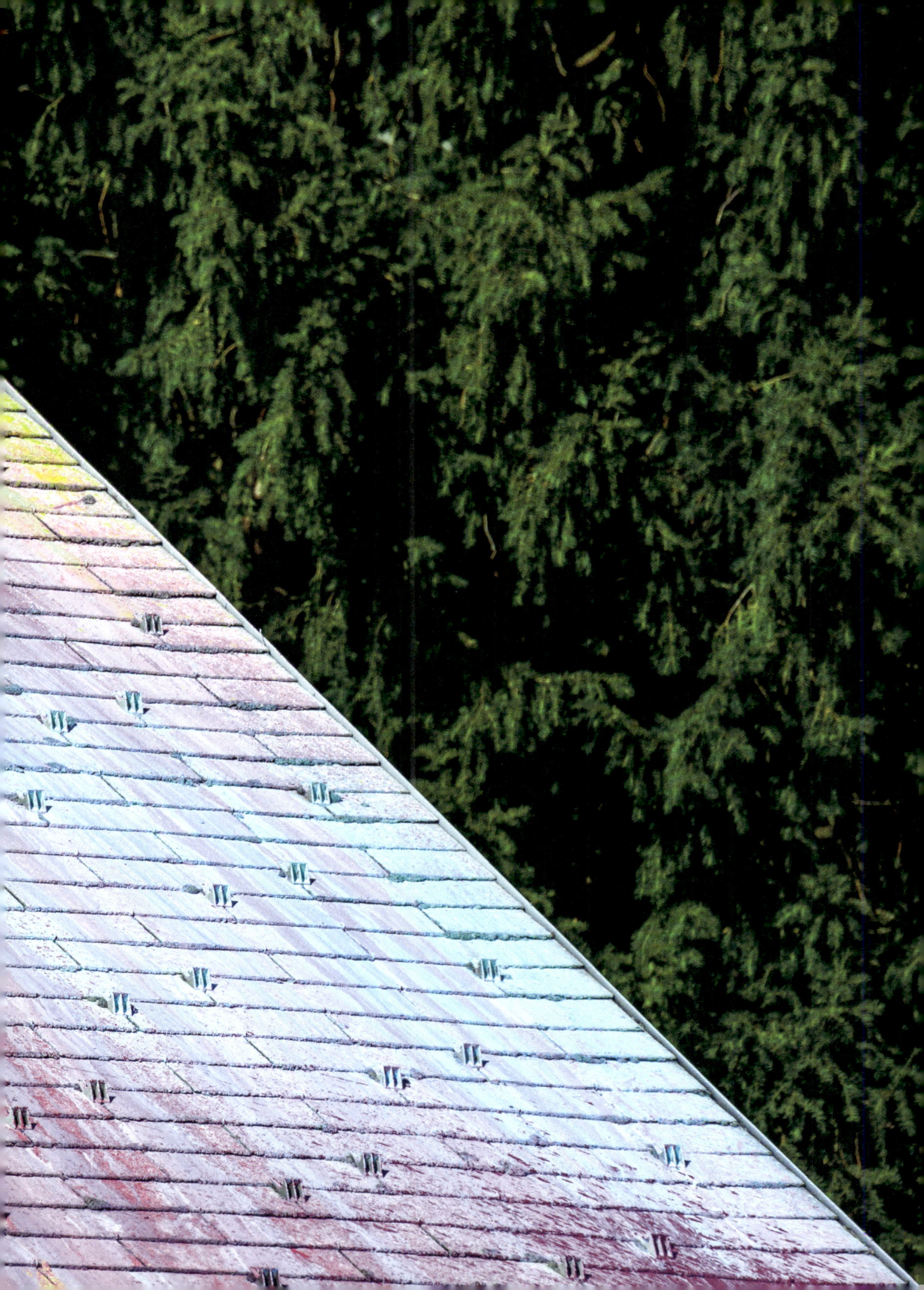

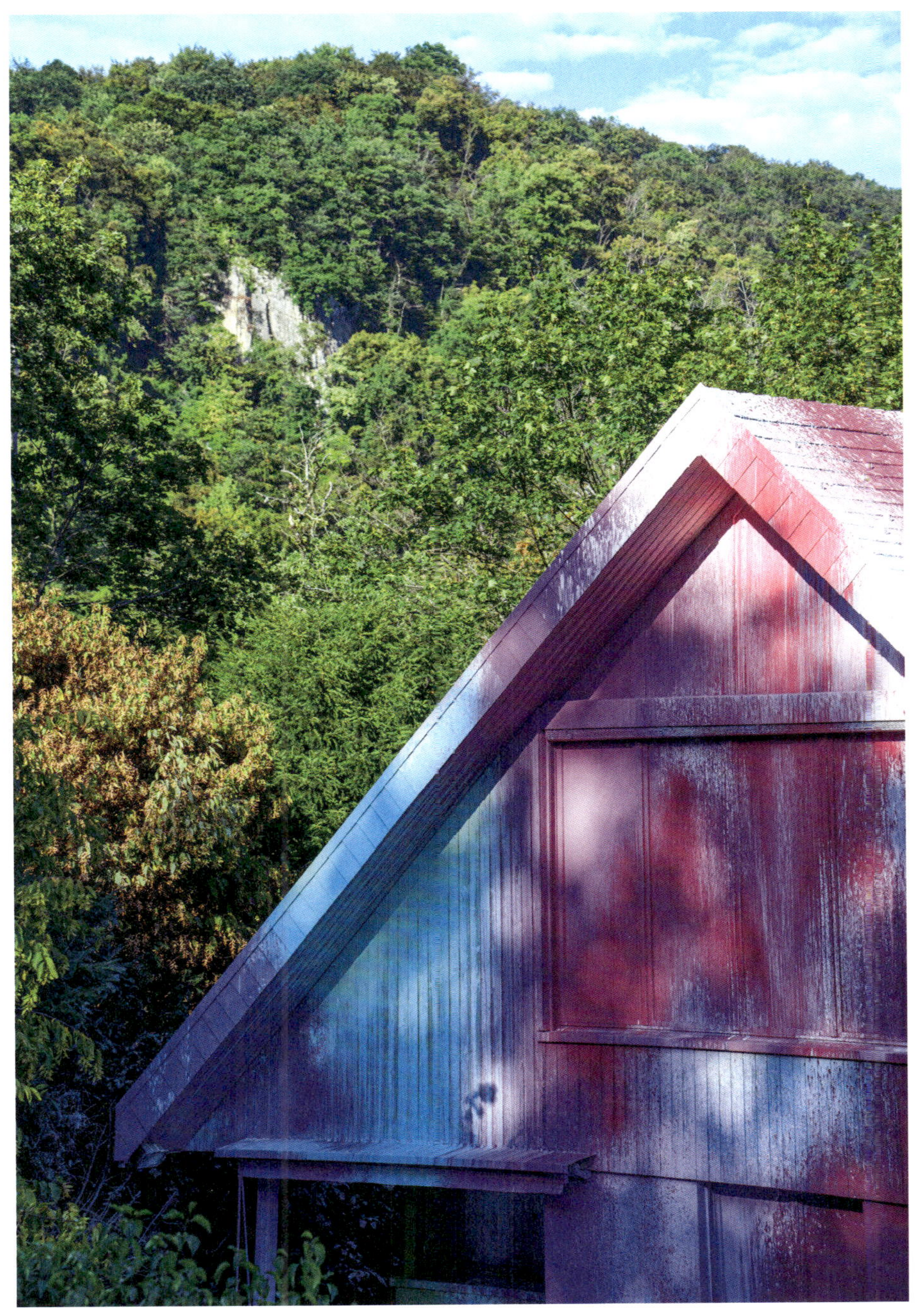

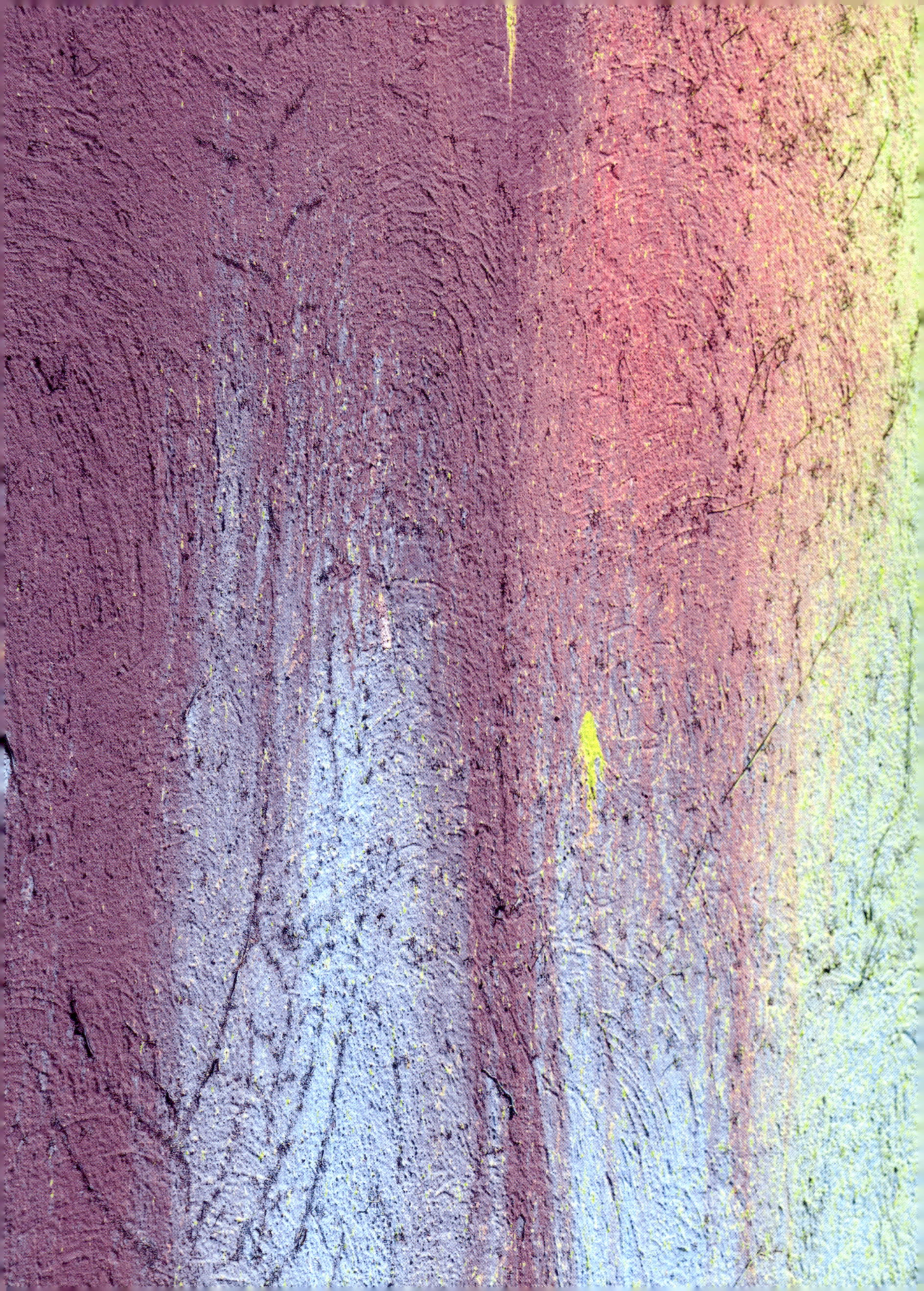

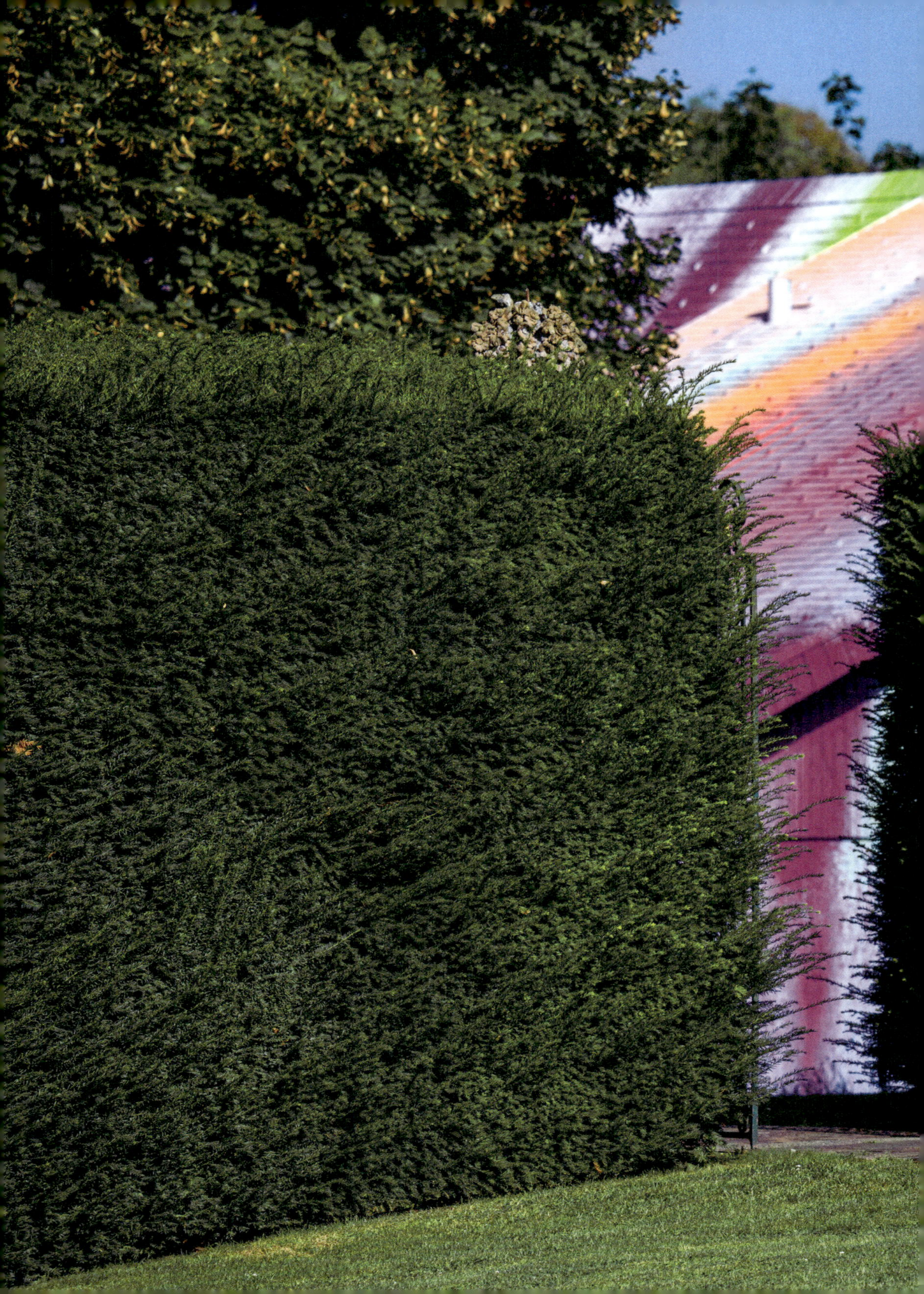

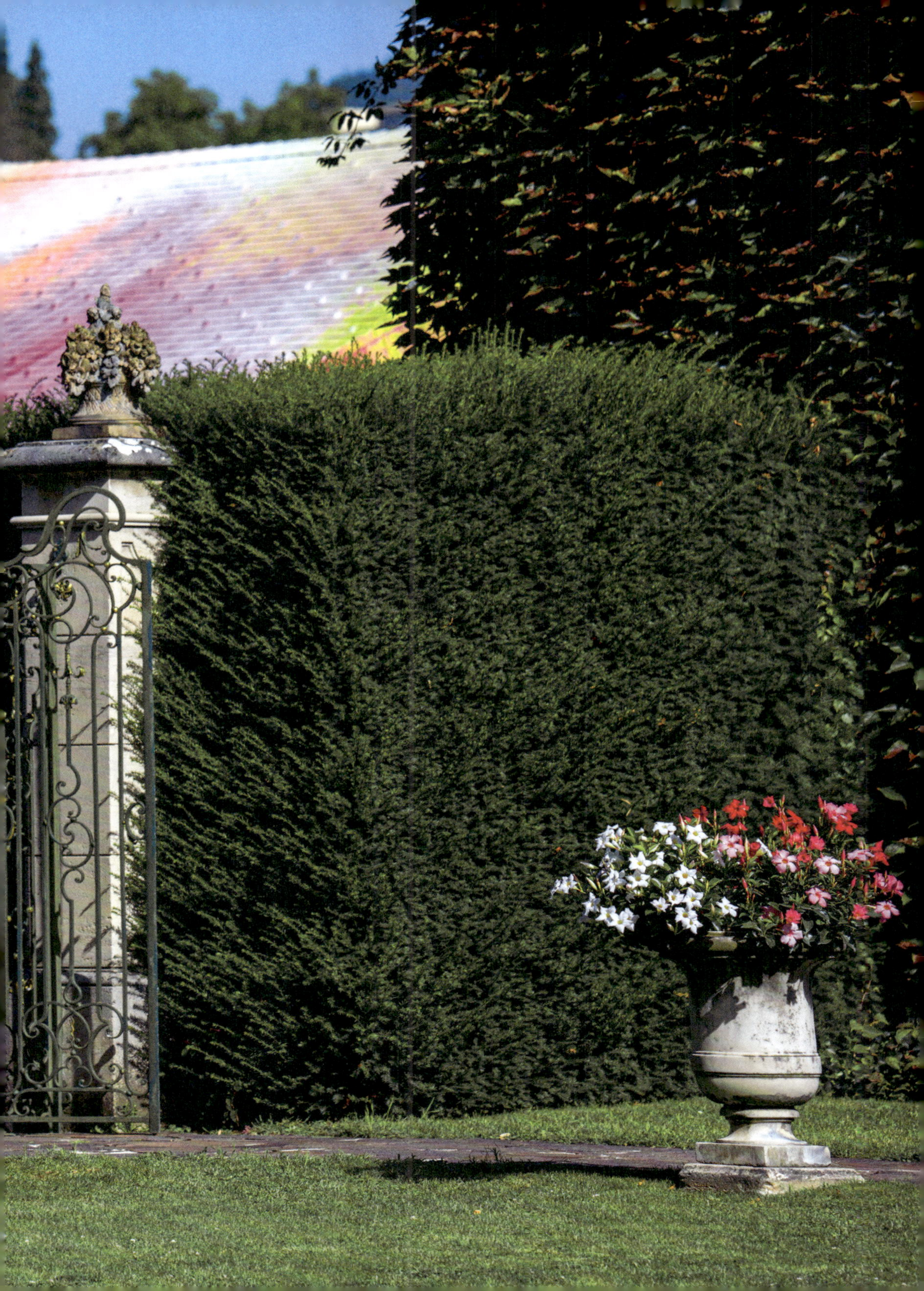

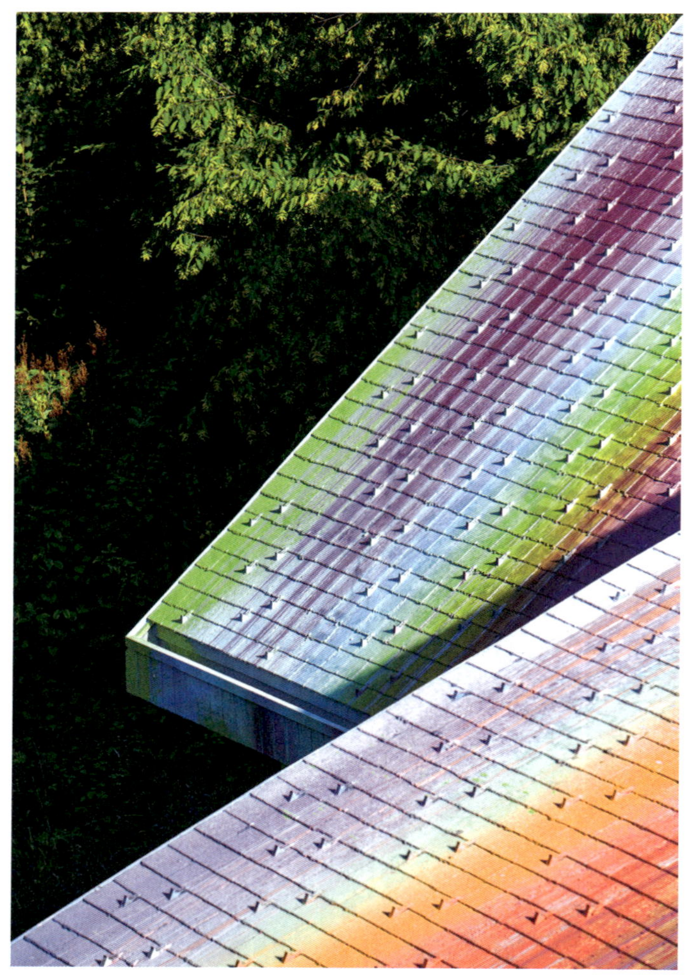

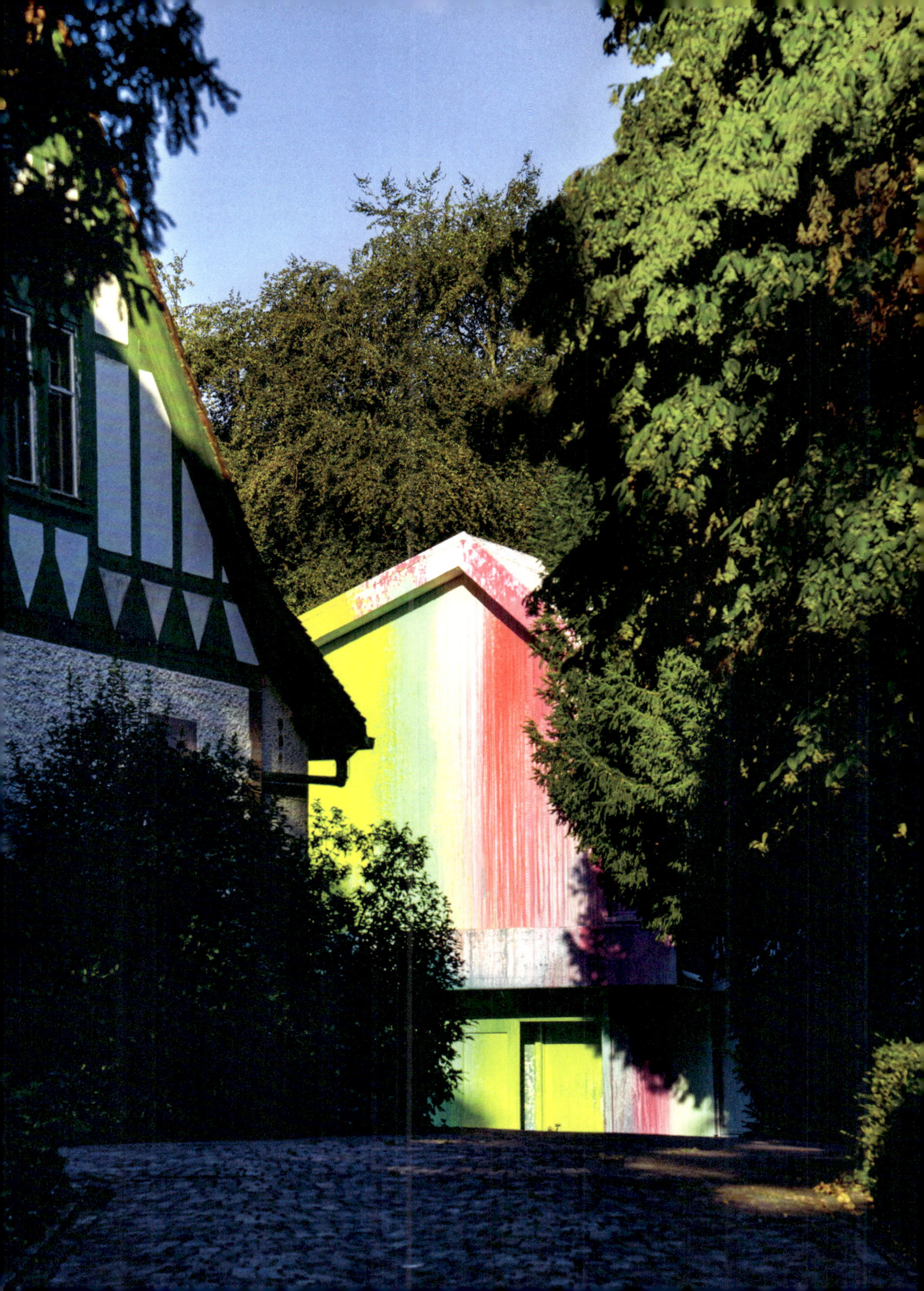

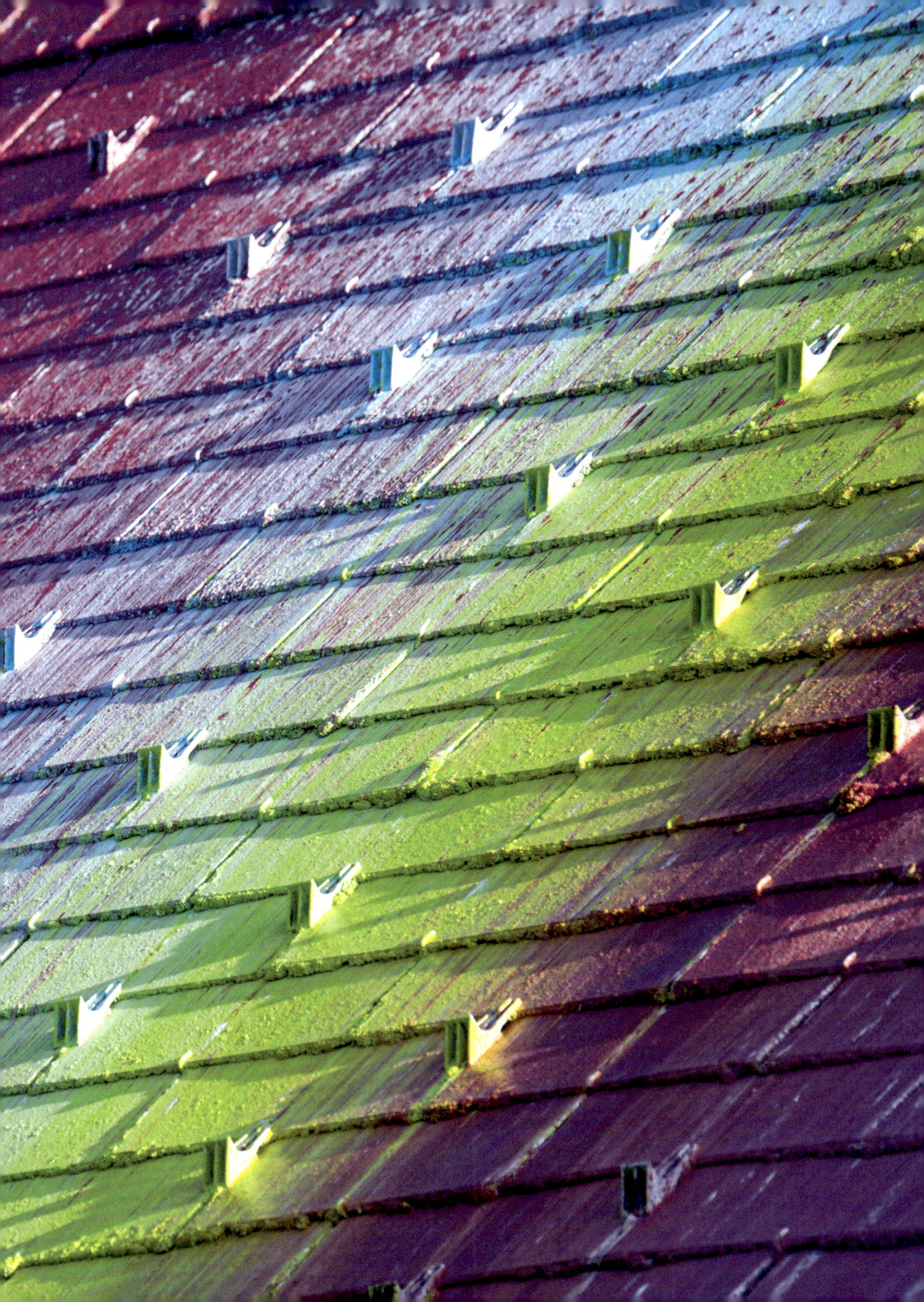

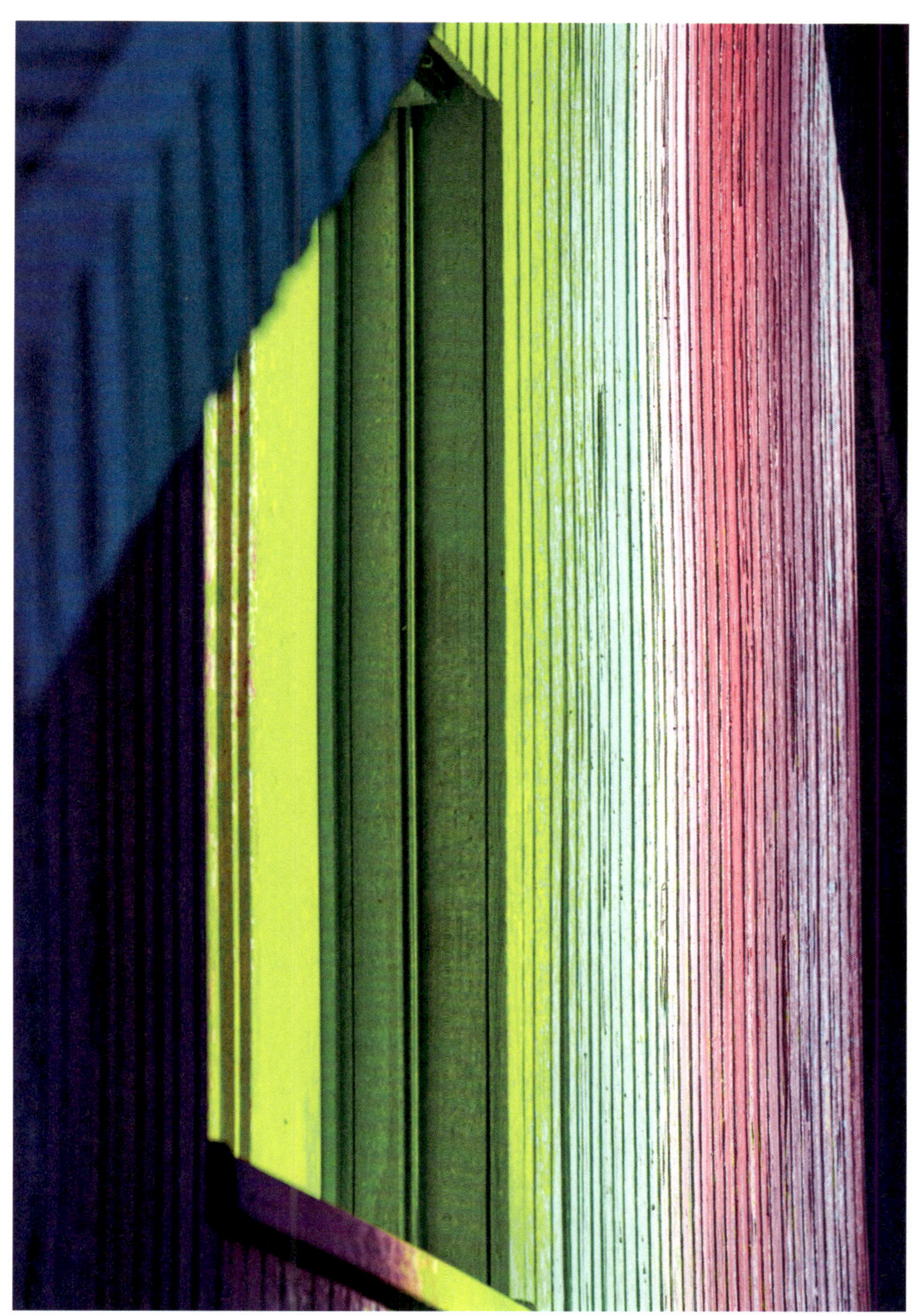

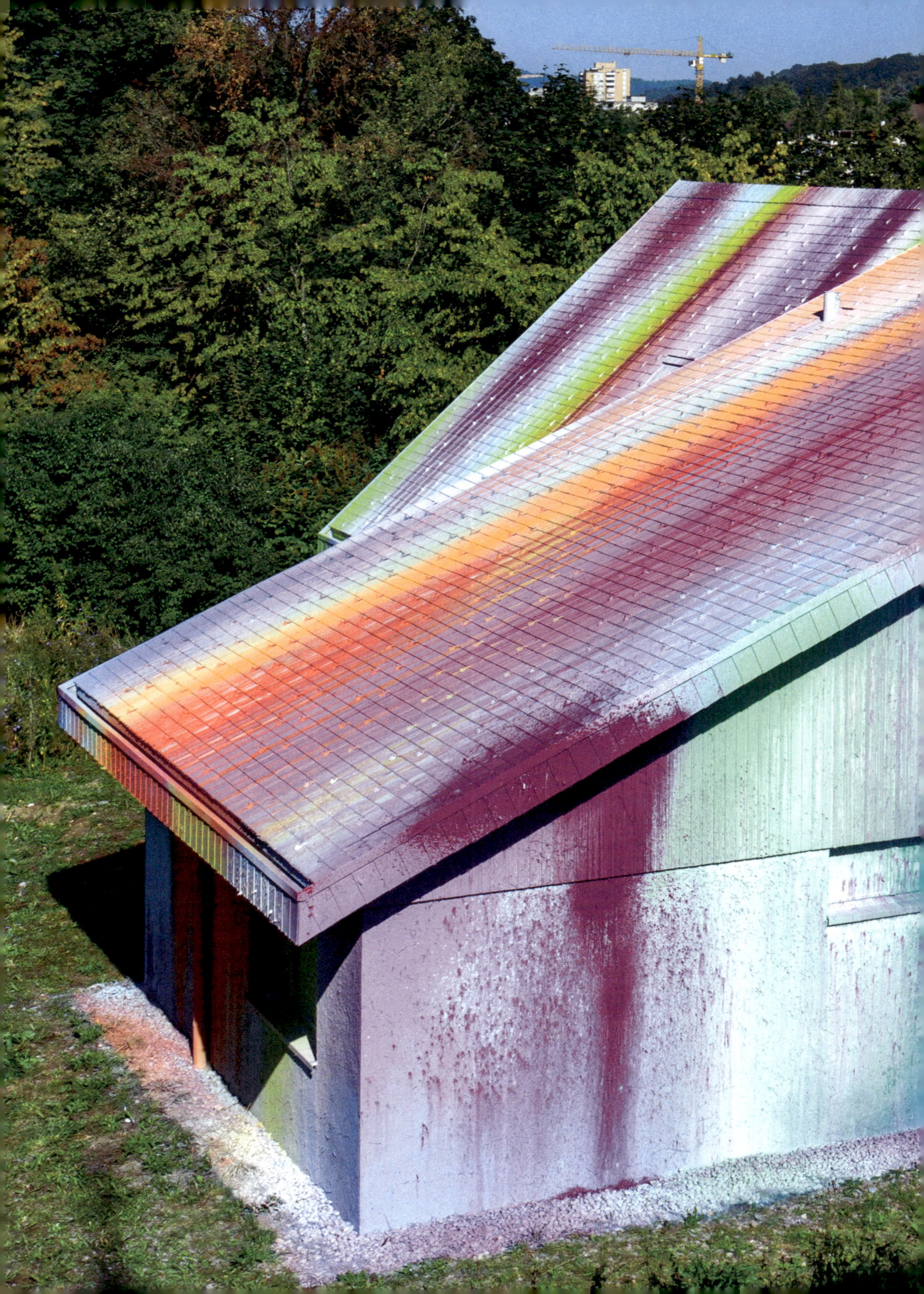

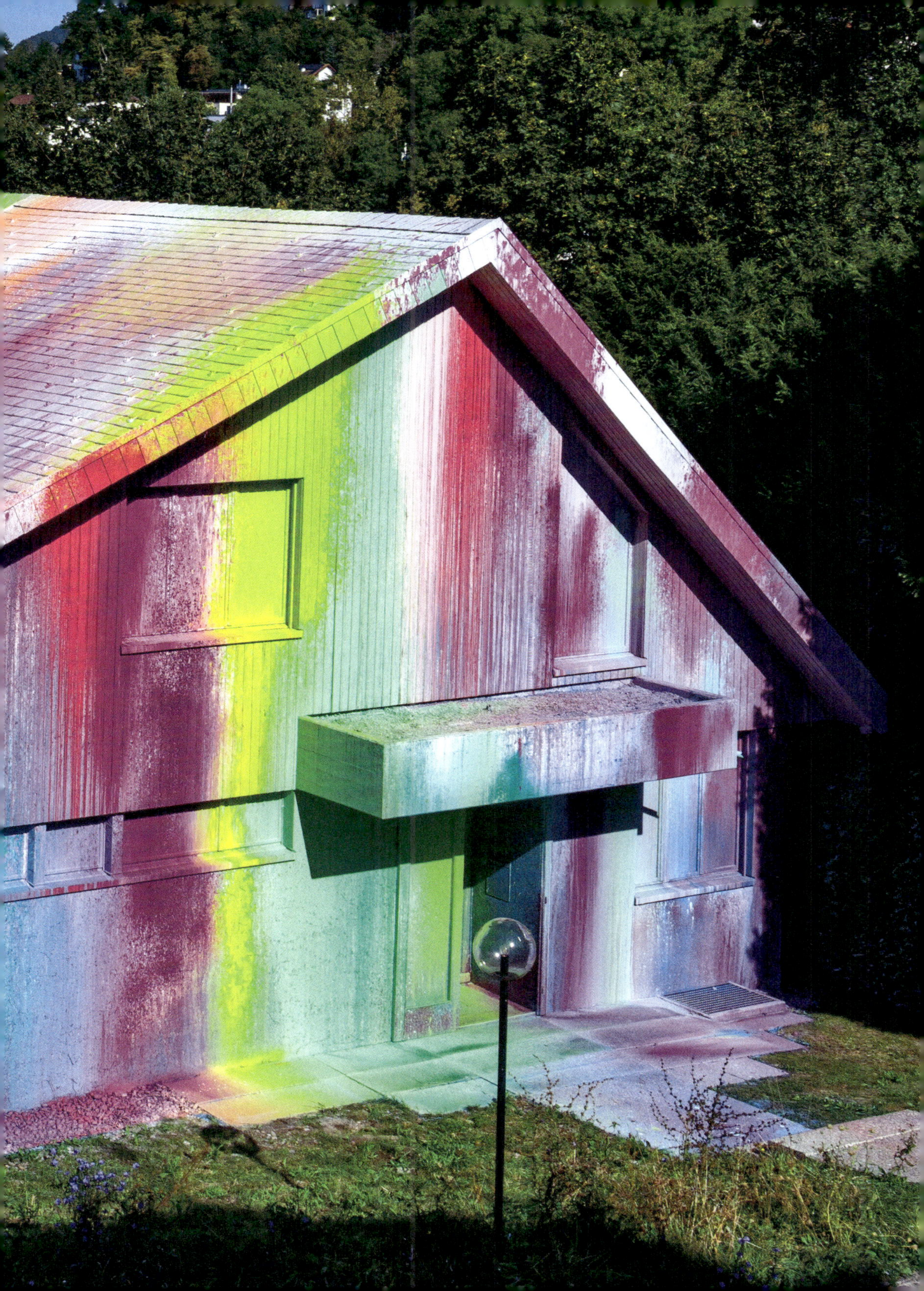

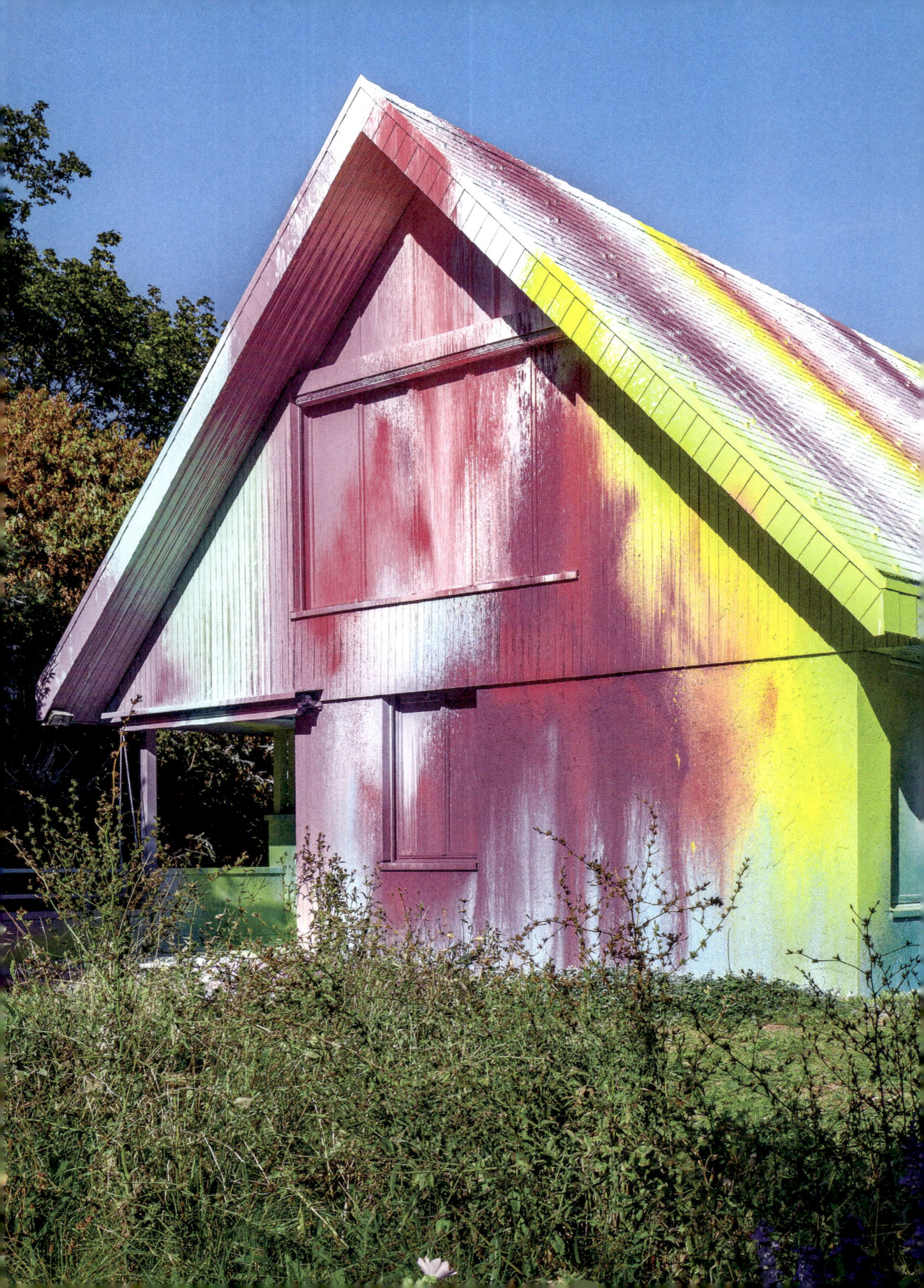

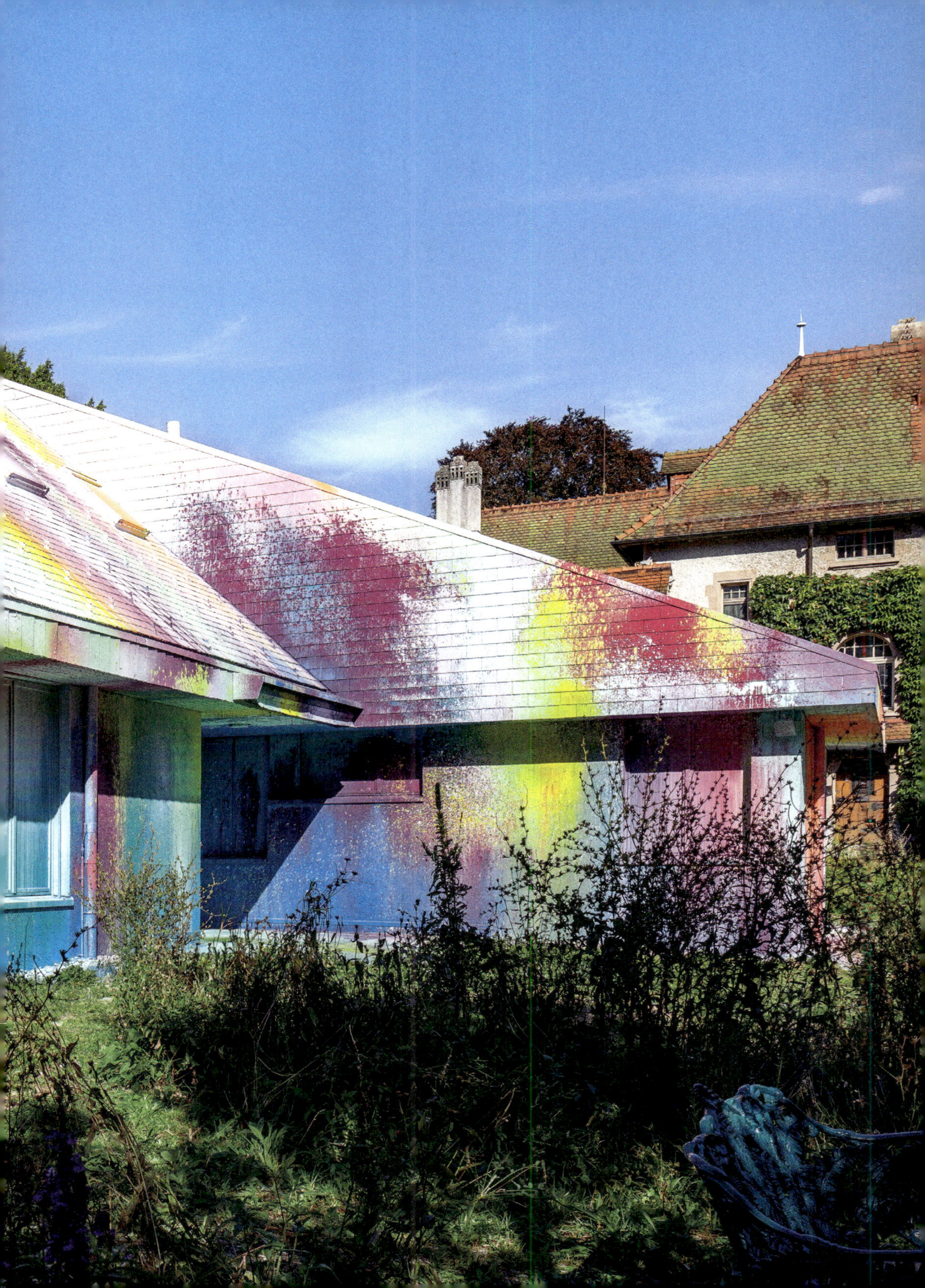

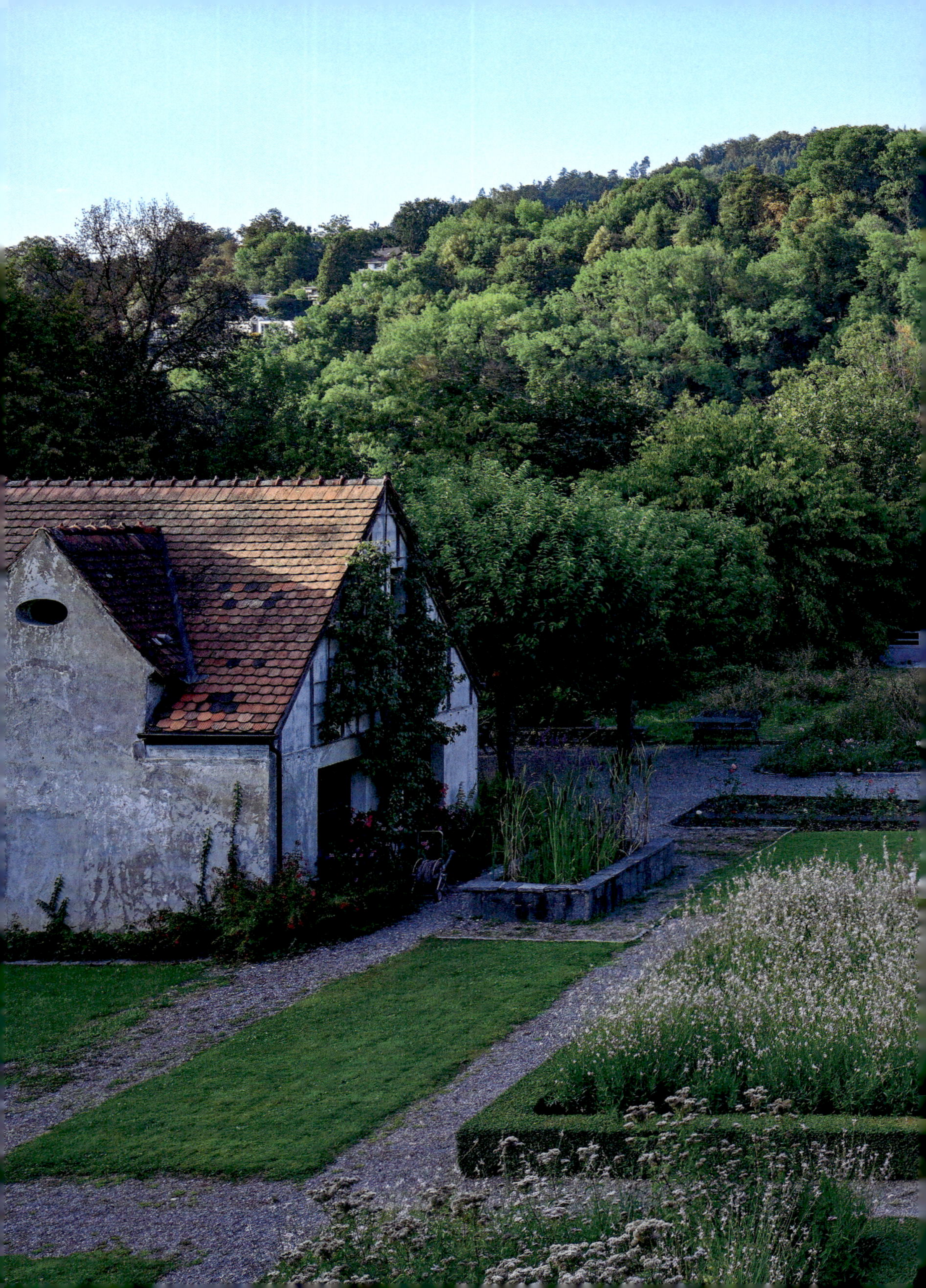

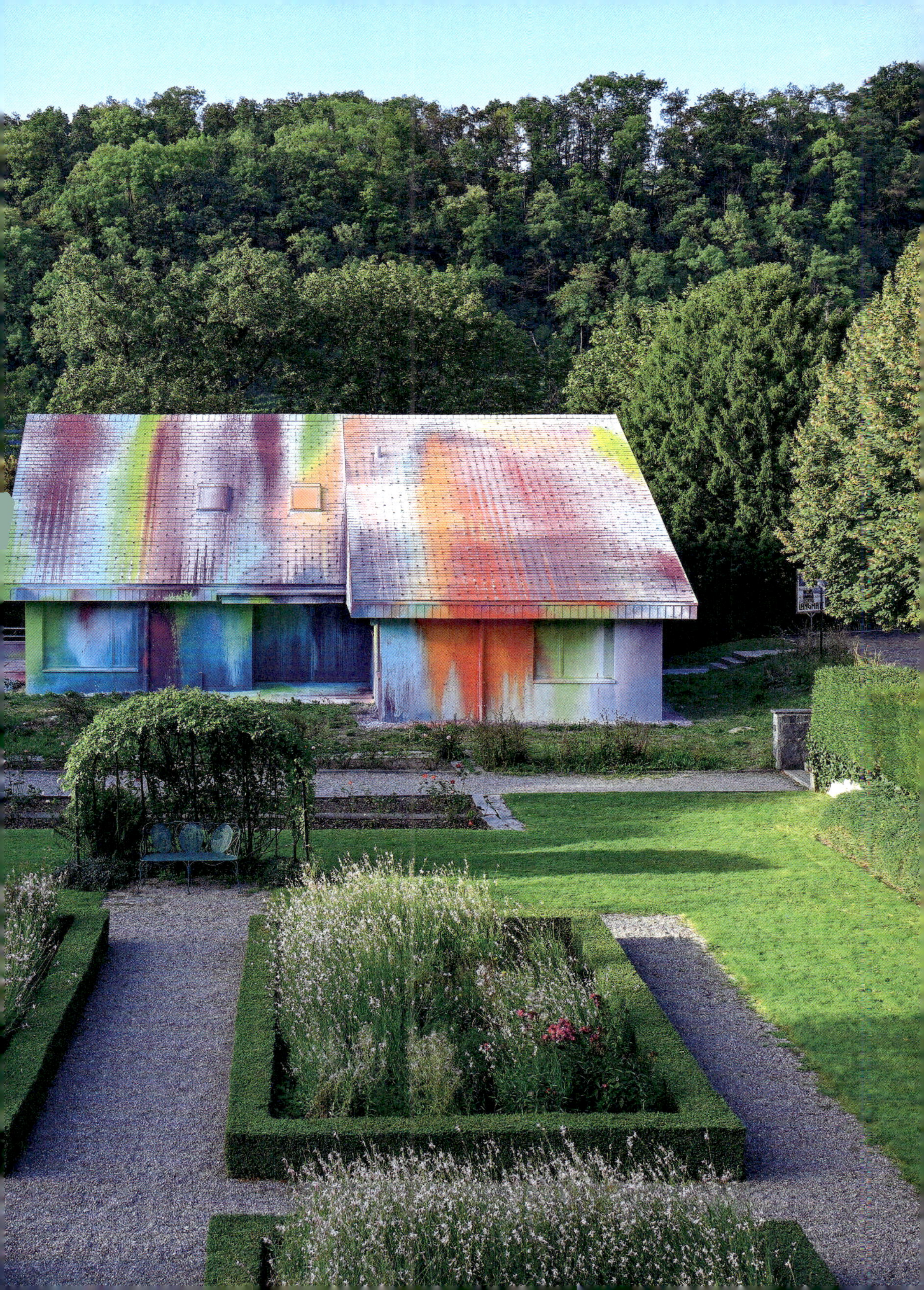

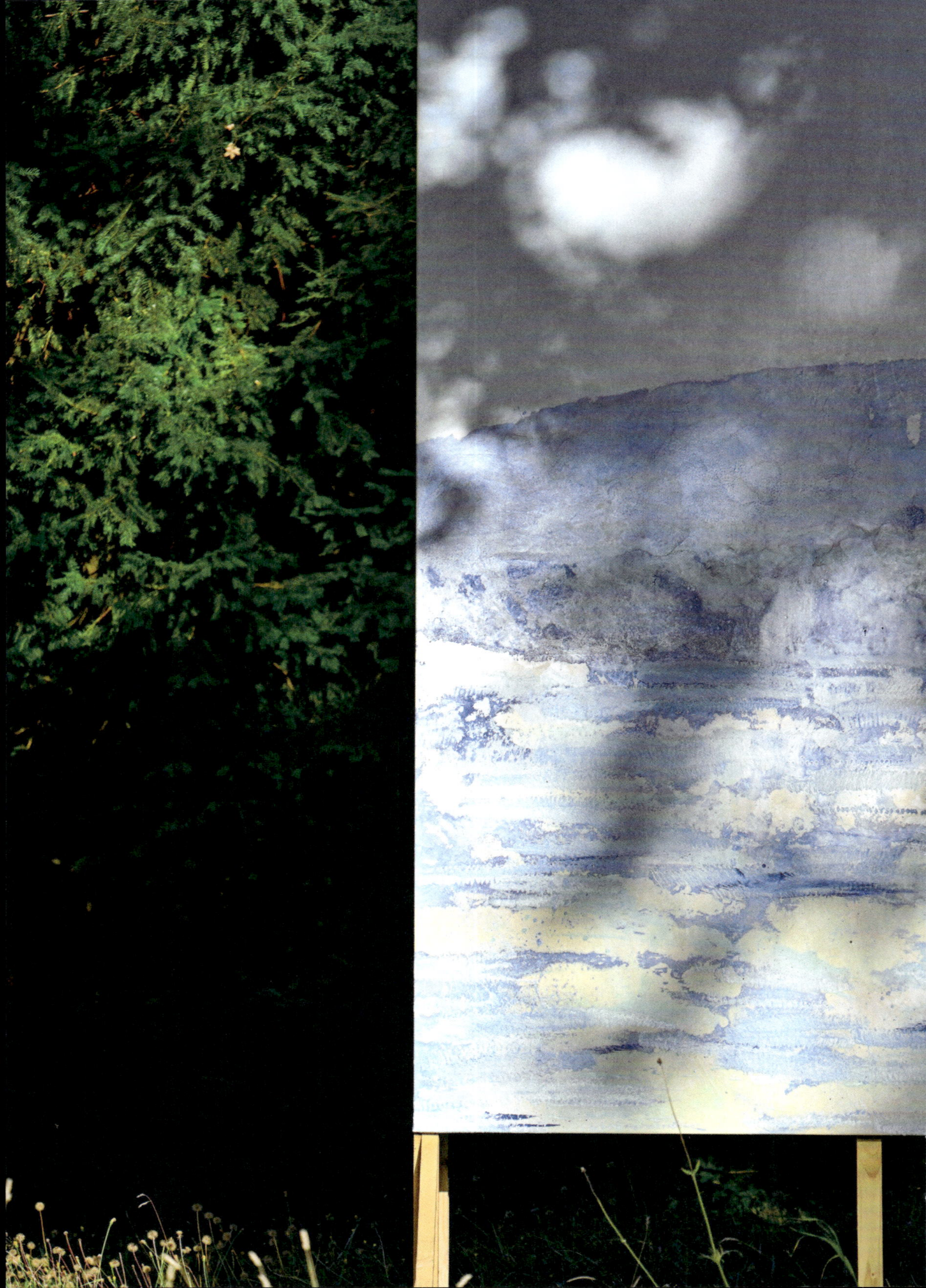

MARKUS STEGMANN

MAGISCHE PRÄSENZ – ZUR MALEREI VON ASH KEATING

MAGICAL PRESENCE: ON THE PAINTING OF ASH KEATING

As soon as you enter the area of the Langmatt, you can see a mysterious structure shining brightly between the dark trees of the avenue. It is as if an enchanted, exotic atoll or a magical, colourfully shimmering iceberg had appeared between the gardener's house and the villa, embedded in the lush greenery of the park: a striking symbol of the power of renewal for the Langmatt. This self-confident artistic statement, with its symbolism that is specific to this sensitive historical site, is one of the reasons why I invited Ash Keating to the Langmatt. Another reason is related to his work on the light and colour effects of nature. As a child, and later as a teenager, he flew in a small plane with his grandmother over the endless expanse of the Australian landscape (see conversation p. 62). The intense colours of the sky and earth had a lasting impact on him. The artist says that he was far more interested in observing nature from the air than in the technology of the airplane or in flying, which he actually wanted to learn to do as a teenager. A potential pilot became an artist. Although this exhibition – Ash Keating's first solo exhibition in Europe – focuses on the spectacular metamorphosis of the caretaker's house, other interesting facets of his work can also be discovered: two large-format triptychs on canvas provide an ideal insight into his painting style. This style is characterised by an energetic colourfulness, a complex painting process in numerous layers and a magical presence. Dazzling, glittering, sparkling surfaces enhance the pellucid reflections of the incoming light, opening up vast spaces for pensive contemplation.

Kaum betritt man das Areal der Langmatt, leuchtet zwischen den dunklen Bäumen der Allee ein rätselhaftes Gebilde hell hervor. Als sei zwischen Gärtnerhaus und Villa ein entrücktes, exotisches Atoll aufgetaucht oder ein magischer, bunt schillernder Eisberg, eingebettet ins üppige Grün des Parks: ein markantes Symbol für die Erneuerungskraft der Langmatt. Dieses selbstbewusste, künstlerische Statement mit seiner spezifischen Symbolik an einem sensiblen historischen Ort ist einer der Gründe, warum ich Ash Keating in die Langmatt eingeladen habe. Ein weiterer liegt in der Nähe seiner Arbeit zu den Licht- und Farbwirkungen der Natur. Als Kind und später als Jugendlicher flog er mit seiner Grossmutter in einem kleinen Flugzeug über die unendliche landschaftliche Weite Australiens (vgl. Gespräch S. 62). Die intensiven Farben zwischen Himmel und Erde haben ihn nachhaltig geprägt. Der Künstler erzählt, die Betrachtung der Natur aus der Luft habe ihn weit mehr interessiert, als die Technik des Flugzeugs oder des Fliegens, das er als Jugendlicher eigentlich erlernen wollte. Aus einem potenziellen Piloten wurde ein Künstler. Wenngleich in der ersten Einzelausstellung Ash Keatings in Europa die spektakuläre Metamorphose des Verwalterhauses im Zentrum steht, sind weitere, interessante Facetten seiner Arbeit zu entdecken: Zwei grossformatige Triptychen auf Leinwand vermitteln einen exemplarischen Einblick in seine Malerei. Sie ist gekennzeichnet von einer energetischen Farbigkeit, einem komplexen Malprozess in zahlreichen Schichten und einer magischen Präsenz. Schillernde, glitzernde, funkelnde Oberflächen steigern die luziden Reflexionen des einfallenden Lichts und öffnen weite Räume für kontemplative Betrachtungen.

Ash Keating lernte die Sammlung der französischen Impressionisten im Museum Langmatt über digitale Abbildungen in hoher Auflösung kennen. Dabei war er von Anfang an besonders von Claude Monets *Eisschollen im Dämmerlicht* (1893, Abb. S. 52) fasziniert. Einerseits aufgrund des Abstraktionsgrades des Bildes, andererseits weil er im aufbrechenden Eis der Seine in der Nähe von Giverny ein Sinnbild für den Klimawandel heute erkennt (vgl. Gespräch S. 67). In seinem Triptychon *Ice Floes Response* (2023, Abb. S. 51), das als Hommage an Monets Bild für die Ausstellung in der Langmatt neu entstanden ist, vergrössert Ash Keating nicht nur die Masse beträchtlich, sondern auch den Abstraktionsgrad. Aus der Nähe betrachtet, verschwindet die Landschaft, und man taucht unweigerlich in fliessende Farbwolken im oberen Bildteil und in die das Licht reflektierenden, horizontal schwebenden Eisschollen im unteren ein. Während die Hügelkette im Hintergrund wie schmelzendes Eis schimmernd zu zerfliessen scheint, verlieren die funkelnden Eisschollen den festen Boden. Fein gemahlenes Glas, als letzte Schicht der Farbe aufgetragen, glitzert vor allem bei direktem Sonnenlicht wie unzählige, winzige Katzenaugen. Eine Landschaft in vielfältiger Auflösung. Ein letzter, traumverlorener Tanz auf der Titanic? Ash Keating platziert seine Abstraktion der Abstraktion von Claude Monet draussen in der Natur, im Park der Langmatt. Die doppelte Entfernung von der Natur kehrt somit wieder zu ihrem Ursprung zurück: ins Herz der Natur. Damit verbunden ist ein aufschlussreicher Kontrast: Während das Bild von Monet bestens geschützt im Inneren des Museums gezeigt wird, ist das Triptychon von Ash Keating draussen verschiedensten Witterungseinflüssen ausgesetzt. Hier die gut gesicherte «Ewigkeit», dort eine Antwort auf diese, welche die Vergänglichkeit bewusst in Kauf nimmt. Ash Keatings Hommage ist daher trotz der grossen Dimensionen und der Präsentation als «Billboards» mit einer bemerkenswerten

Ash Keating first became acquainted with the French Impressionist artworks collection at the Museum Langmatt in the form of high-resolution digital illustrations. From the very beginning, he was particularly fascinated by Claude Monet's *Ice Floes at Twilight* (1893, fig. p. 52). This was because of the degree of abstraction of the picture on the one hand, and on the other hand because he recognises a symbol of the climate change of today in the breaking ice of the Seine near Giverny (see interview p. 66/67). In his triptych *Ice Floes Response* (2023, fig. p. 51), which was created for the exhibition at the Langmatt as a tribute to Monet's painting, Ash Keating not only increases the degree of mass considerably, but also the degree of abstraction. Seen at close quarters, the landscape disappears, and one is irresistibly immersed in the flowing clouds of colour in the upper part of the picture and in the reflective, horizontally floating ice floes in the lower part. While the chain of hills in the background seems to dissolve like melting ice, the sparkling ice floes lose their solid ground. Finely ground glass, applied in the last layer of paint, glitters like countless, tiny cat's-eyes, especially in direct sunlight. A landscape engaged in multiple forms of dissolution. A final, dreamy dance on the Titanic.

Ash Keating places his abstraction of Claude Monet's abstraction outside and in a natural setting, in the Langmatt park. Doubly distanced from nature, it is thus returned to its origin: to the heart of nature. This induces a revealing contrast: while the painting by Monet is displayed inside the Museum where it is well-protected, the triptych by Ash Keating is outdoors and exposed to a wide variety of weather conditions. The one is well-secured and 'eternal'; the other represents a response to it, consciously accepting its transience. Ash Keating's homage therefore possesses a remarkable modesty, despite its large dimensions and 'billboard' presentation. Viewed from a certain distance, the line of hills depicted in the picture and the line of the real hills in the park exist in a well-balanced relationship to each other. The chosen location allows the artwork to be effective both at a long distance and at close quarters. Ash Keating's exploration of *Ice Floes at Twilight* has since led him to create a new, extensive group of works. The degree of abstractilon is, once again, significantly increased, with the landscape's outlines entirely receding.

Bescheidenheit verbunden. Die abgebildete Hügellinie im Bild und die reale im Park – aus gewisser Distanz betrachtet – stehen in einem wohl ausbalancierten Verhältnis gegenläufig zueinander. Der gewählte Ort ist sowohl auf Fern- als auch auf Nahwirkung angelegt. Die Auseinandersetzung mit den *Eisschollen im Dämmerlicht* führte Ash Keating mittlerweile zu einer neuen, umfangreichen Werkgruppe. Der Abstraktionsgrad ist nochmals deutlich gesteigert, so dass landschaftliche Umrisse vollends zurücktreten.

In der Ausstellung zeigt sich Ash Keating jedoch nicht nur als ein Meister des grossen Formats und der selbstbewussten Geste, sondern beweist auch die souveräne Beherrschung «leiser Töne». Das explosive Haus Germann draussen lässt die subtilen, romantischen Wirkungen drinnen in der Gemäldegalerie nicht vermuten. Das Triptychon *GSR 15_2022 Triptych* (Abb. S. 56) aus der Werkserie *Gravity System Response* tritt in zarten, hellen Rosétönen in Dialog mit den Impressionisten der Sammlung, die im Rahmen der Ausstellung *Forever Young* zu sehen sind. Der Werktitel verweist auf die der Schwerkraft folgenden, vertikal fliessenden Farben. Auf den ersten Blick sind die Kontraste zwischen den relativ kleinformatigen, gegenständlichen Impressionisten und den drei grossformatigen, hell leuchtenden Bildtafeln relativ gross. Plötzlich wirken die sonst so strahlenden Impressionisten ein wenig abgedunkelt. Die Stirnwand der Gemäldegalerie ist eine prominente Bühne, auf der *GSR 15_2022 Triptych* bei aller subtilen Fragilität der zarten Rosévaleurs eine überraschende Ruhe und Präsenz ausstrahlt. Aus der Nähe betrachtet, sind die Leinwände von einem subtilen Glitzern und Funkeln überzogen, was sich durch die Verwendung von irisierenden Pigmenten erklärt. Die graue Stoffbespannung der Wand verstärkt als relativ dunkler Hintergrund den Kontrast und steigert zusätzlich die Leuchtkraft des Triptychons. Auf den ersten Blick nimmt eine zarte, fast magische Ästhetik gefangen, doch diese scheint ambivalent zu sein, denn bald schon macht sich auch eine leicht toxische Ausstrahlung bemerkbar. Die Leuchtkraft der Bildtafeln besitzt eine überstrahlende, subtil glimmende Energie. Das macht den Kern dieser Arbeit aus: Der schmale Grat, der Kippmoment zwischen zwei unterschiedlichen emotionalen Polen. Je nach Blickwinkel und Stimmungslage kann das eine rasch in das andere umschlagen und wieder zurück.

Ohne Furcht vor ästhetischen Wirkungen wandelt Ash Keating auf einem Grat zwischen kontemplativer, romantischer Schönheit und leicht toxischer Intensität. Er kennt keine Berührungsängste mit malerischer Schönheit, wie manch andere Kunstschaffende der Gegenwart. Immer noch ein heikles und verfängliches Thema, das Stoff für emotionale Diskussionen liefert. Offensichtlich wiegt nach wie vor das Credo der Moderne schwer, wonach Kunst auf keinen Fall «schön» sein dürfe, sonst würde sie sich dem Vorwurf der «Dekoration» und somit der «Oberflächlichkeit» aussetzen. So fraglos berechtigt der teilweise erbittert geführte Kampf der Moderne im 20. Jahrhundert auch war, um sich von überkommenen, akademischen Schönheitsidealen zu befreien, so fragwürdig ist eine solche Haltung, wenn sie sich dogmatisch verhärtet. Davon abgesehen, bezieht zeitgenössische Kunst nach

In the exhibition, however, Keating not only shows himself to be a master of large-format artworks and confident gestures, but also demonstrates his assured mastery of 'quiet tones'. The explosive Haus Germann outside gives no hint of the subtle, romantic effects inside the *Gemäldegalerie*. With its delicate, light pink tones, the triptych entitled *GSR 15_2022 Triptych* (fig. p. 56) from the artwork series titled *Gravity System Response* engages in dialogue with the Impressionist artworks in the collection (which can be seen as part of the exhibition *Forever Young*). The title of the artwork refers to the vertically flowing paints, which follow gravity. At first glance, the differences between the relatively small-format, representational Impressionist artworks and the three large-format, brightly-shining panels appear profound. Suddenly, the otherwise radiant Impressionist artworks appear to be a little darkened. Displayed on the prominent stage provided by the front wall of the *Gemäldegalerie*, the *GSR 15_2022 Triptych* exudes a surprising calm and presence despite all the subtle fragility of the delicate rose colour values. Viewed at close quarters, the canvases are seen to be covered with a subtle glitter and sparkle: this is explained by the use of iridescent pigments. The relatively dark background provided by the grey fabric covering of the wall enhances the contrast and additionally increases the luminosity of the triptych. At first glance, the delicate, almost magical aesthetic is captivating, but there appears to be a certain ambivalence about it, because soon a slightly toxic charisma becomes noticeable. The luminosity of the panels has a subtly glowing energy that outshines other light sources. This is the core of this work: the fine line, the tipping point between two different emotional poles. Depending on point of view and mood, the one can swiftly be turned into the other, only to be reversed again.

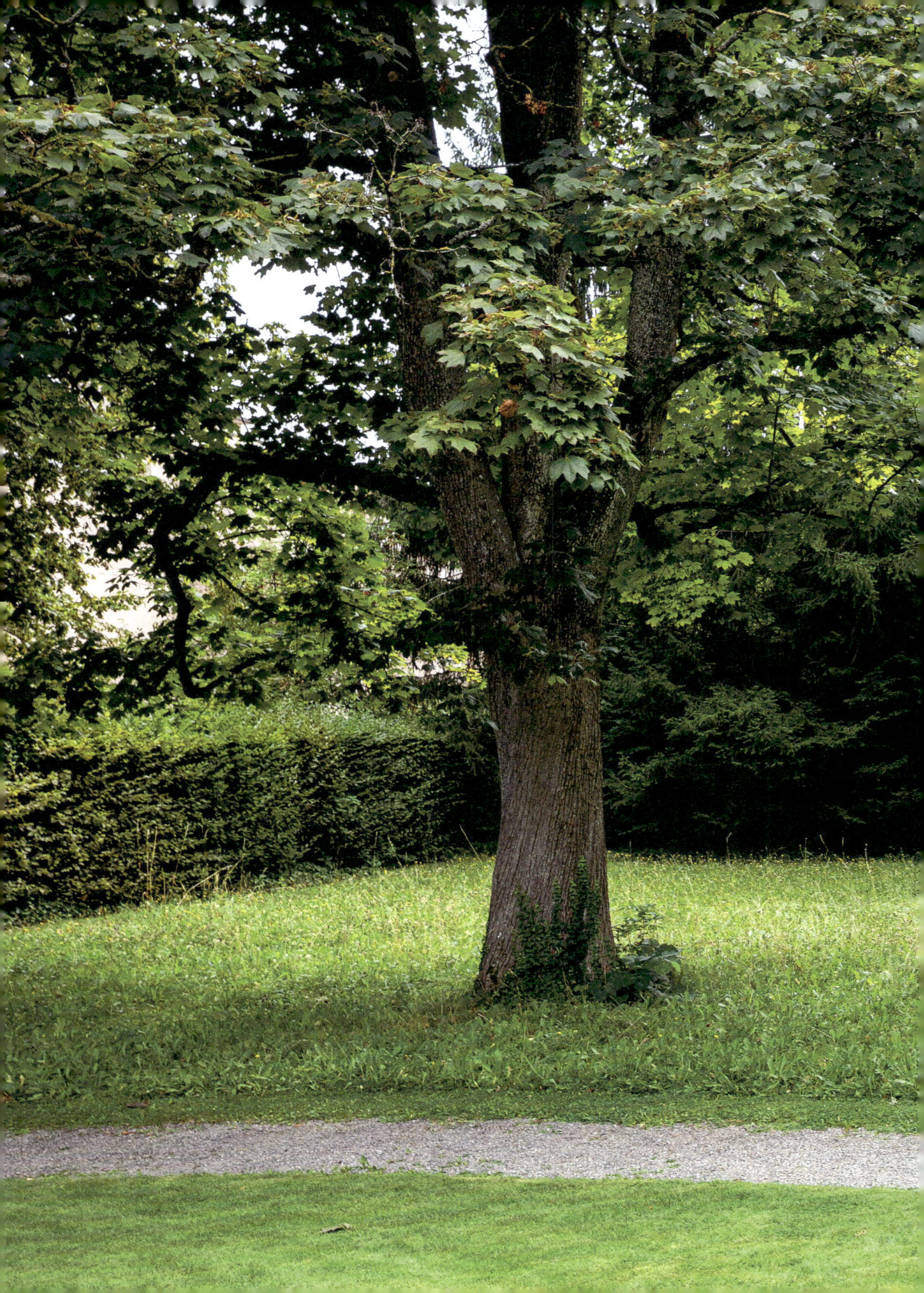

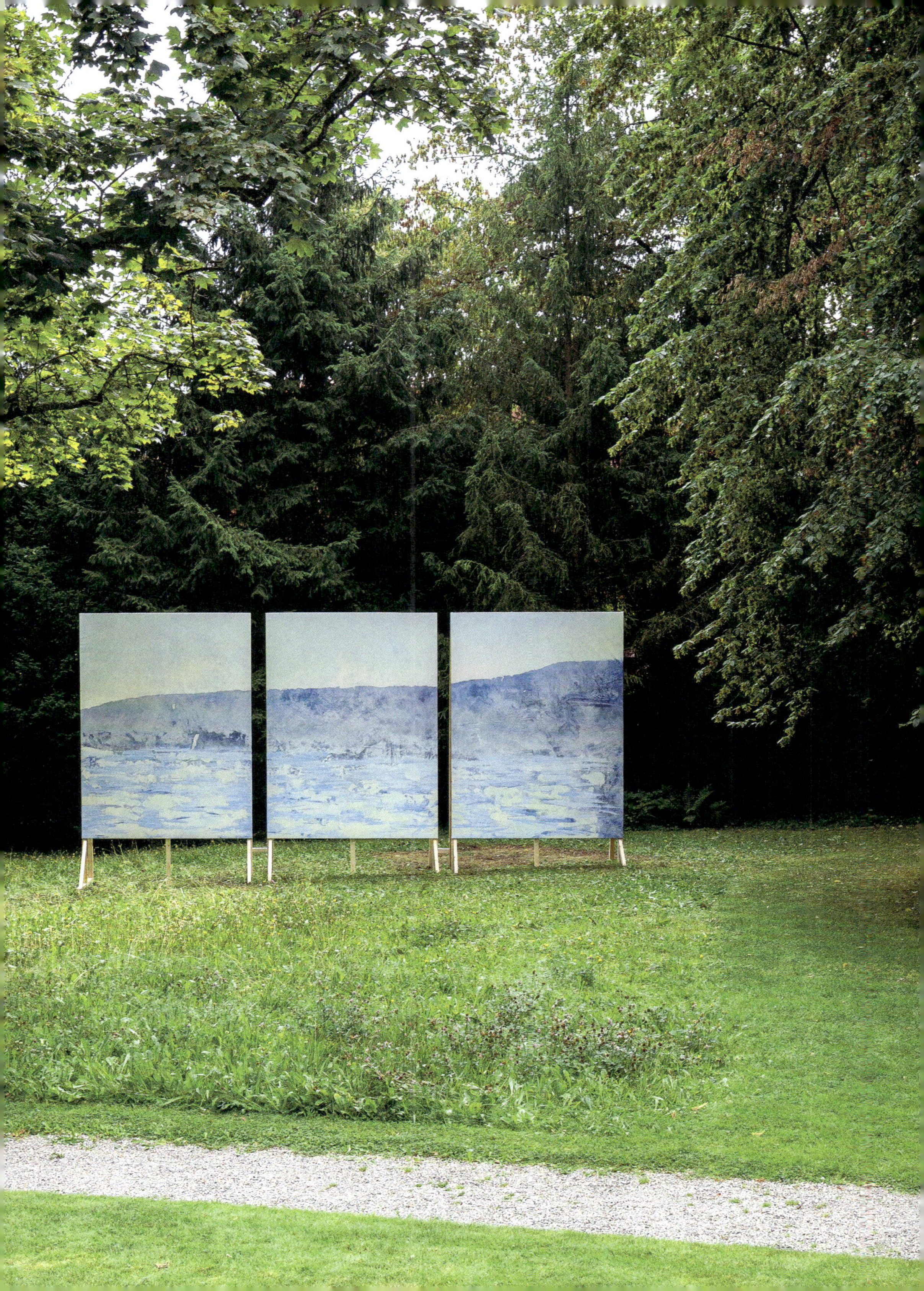

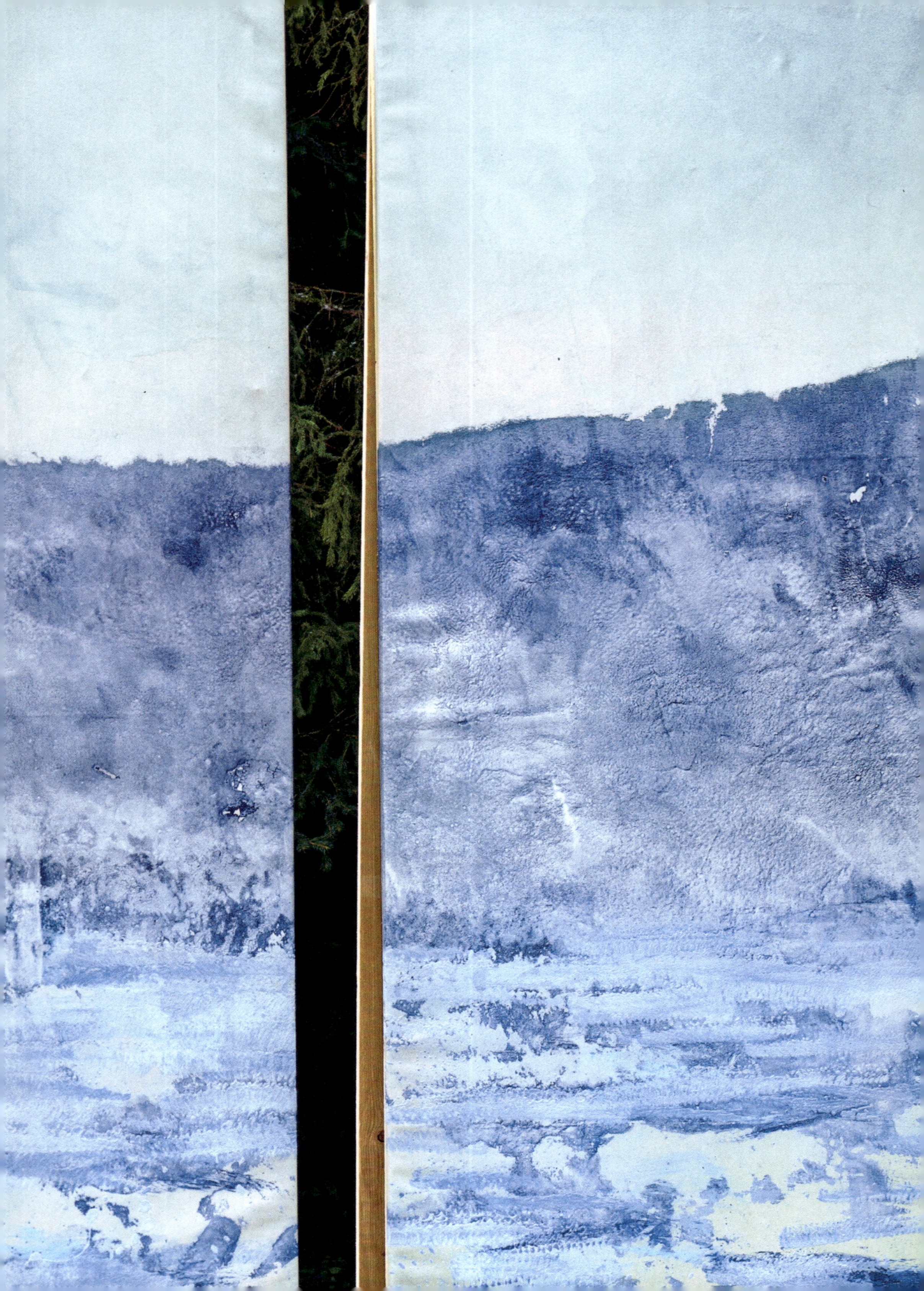

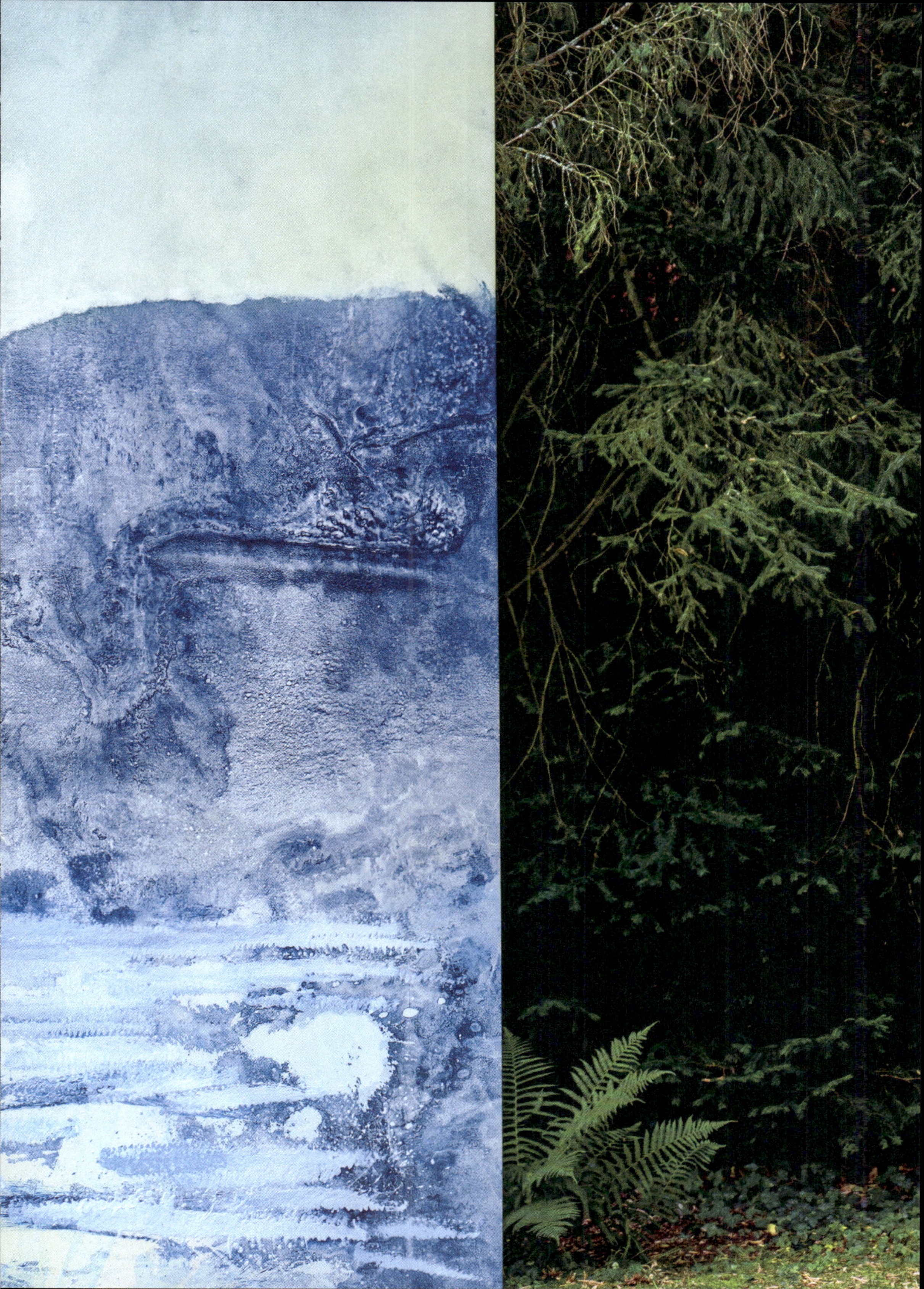

Without fear of aesthetic effects,
Ash Keating walks a fine line between
contemplative, romantic beauty and
slightly toxic intensity. He has no fear
of making contact with painterly
beauty, like many other contemporary
artists. This remains a delicate and
intricate topic that provides material
for emotional discussions. Obviously,
the credo of modernism – according
to which art may not be 'beautiful' under
any circumstances, lest it expose itself to the accusation of 'decoration'
and thus of 'superficiality' – still carries
weight. As unquestionably justified
as modernism in the twentieth century
was in its sometimes bitter struggle
to free itself from outdated, academic
ideals of beauty, such an attitude is
questionable when it hardens into
dogma. Quite apart from that, contemporary art still derives a significant
part of its power of renewal from coun-
ter-cyclical behaviour. What seems
to be an inviolable taboo to one generation of artists is often rediscovered –
recombined and illuminated from an
unusual perspective – by the next.
Every generation of artists has the right
to form their own idea of reality, to de-
velop their own perspective and artistic
language. To put it bluntly, these are
backgrounds and contexts that are relevant to the perception of Ash Keating's painting. Undaunted, he follows a
path that is still the subject of heated
debate, and puts the question of beauty
to the test. The Langmatt as a historical ensemble is a special place that
undoubtedly possesses considerable
aesthetic and atmospheric charms:
the lush blooming flowers in the park,
the lavishly decorated historic interior
of the villa, the rich, seductive colour
palette of the Impressionist artworks.
It is precisely in places like this that
questions arise concerning beauty and
its legitimacy and perhaps even its
necessity in a broader context: the per-
meability of the historical structure
between the park outside and the Impressionist depictions of nature
inside is a rich basis for reflection.

Ice Floes Response, 2023
Acryl, Pigment und Glasperlen
auf Baumwollgewebe /
Acrylic, pigment, and glass beads
on cotton fabric
ca. / approx. 300 × 690 cm
(je / each 300 × 220 cm)

wie vor einen erheblichen Teil ihrer Erneuerungskraft aus einem antizyklischen Verhalten. Das, was
einer Generation von Kunstschaffenden als un-
antastbares Tabu erscheint, wird oftmals von der
nachfolgenden als Thema neu entdeckt, aufgebro-
chen und aus einem ungewohnten Blickwinkel be-
leuchtet. Jede Generation an Kunstschaffenden
hat das gute Recht, sich eine eigene Vorstellung
von der Wirklichkeit zu bilden, ihre eigene Sicht-
weise und künstlerische Sprache zu entwickeln.
Das sind – etwas salopp zusammengefasst – Hintergründe und Zusammenhänge, die für die Wahrnehmung der Malerei von Ash Keating relevant
sind. Unerschrocken beschreitet er einen immer
noch kontrovers diskutierten Weg und stellt die
Frage nach der Schönheit auf den Prüfstand. Die
Langmatt als historisches Ensemble ist ein be-
sonderer Ort, der fraglos erhebliche ästhetische
und atmosphärische Reize besitzt: die üppig blü-
henden Blumen im Park, das aufwändig dekorierte
historische Interieur der Villa, die reiche, verfüh-
rerische Farbpalette der Impressionisten. Gerade
an einem solchen Ort stellen sich Fragen nach der
Schönheit, ihrer Legitimation, vielleicht sogar ihrer
Notwendigkeit in einem erweiterten Kontext: Die
Durchlässigkeit des historischen Gefüges zwischen dem Park draussen und den Naturdarstel-
lungen des Impressionismus drinnen ist eine er-
giebige Basis der Reflexion.

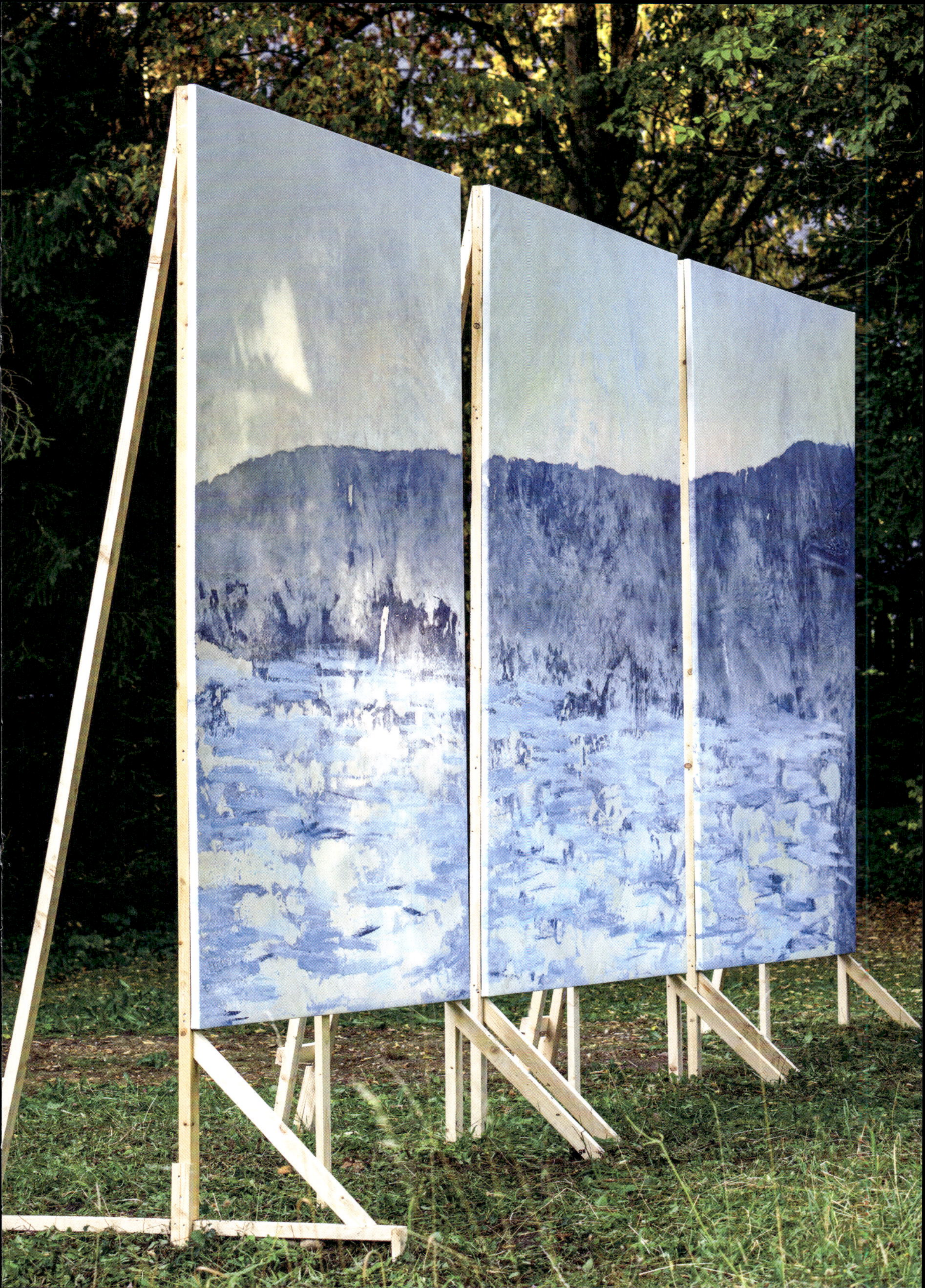

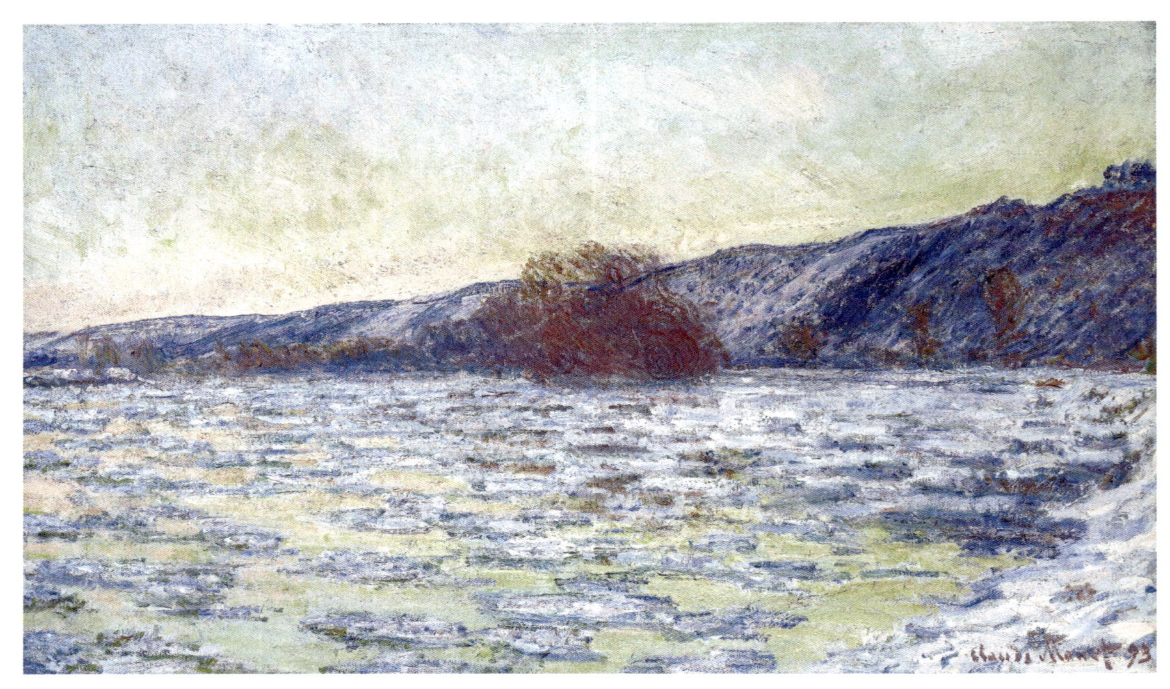

Claude Monet
Eisschollen im Dämmerlicht /
Ice Floes at Twilight, 1893
Öl auf Leinwand / Oil on canvas,
60 × 100 cm
Museum Langmatt, Baden

Um die künstlerische Sprache von Ash Keating zu kontextualisieren, ist ein Blick in die jüngere Kunstgeschichte aufschlussreich. Die grossformatigen *Drip Paintings* von Jackson Pollock (1912–1956) stehen ab 1946 für eine radikale Befreiung des Action Painting von tradierten Kompositionsvorstellungen, indem der Zufall und ein performativer Malprozess an der Entstehung der Bilder massgeblich beteiligt waren. Morris Louis (1912–1962) liess in seinen *Veil Paintings* ab 1954 Farbe in bunten Valeurs an den Rändern der Leinwände vertikal herabfliessen. Auch er verzichtete auf den Pinsel und somit auf Handschriftlichkeit und gab durch das Fliessen der Farbe ein Stück Kontrolle aus der Hand, setzte jedoch als ein Vertreter des Color Field Painting stärker auf ästhetische Wirkungen. Hermann Nitsch (1938–2022) wiederum schleuderte ab 1960 in vehementen, öffentlichen Akten rote Farbe als «Schüttungen» auf die Leinwände. Diese Arbeiten stehen in ganz anderen, gewissermassen kultischen Zusammenhängen seines Orgien-Mysterien-Theaters. Der Schock des Zweiten Weltkriegs, die als dringend notwendig erlebte Befreiung und Erneuerung der Malerei, die scharfe Ablehnung der politisch missbrauchten Figuration und die Lust, neue, experimentelle Wege zu gehen, sind für diese Positionen prägend. Ganz andere künstlerische Hintergründe finden sich in den letzten Jahrzehnten beispielsweise in den vertikal fliessenden Bildern von Pat Steir (*1940) und John M. Armleder (*1948) oder den grossformatigen, malerischen Environments von Katharina Grosse (*1961): Die Malerei von Steir und Armleder besitzt eine konzeptionelle Ausgangslage, jene von Grosse eine konstruktive beziehungsweise dekonstruktivistische. Ash Keating hingegen bezieht seine Impulse aus der Landschaft Australiens. Die

In placing Keating's artistic language in context, a look at recent art history is enlightening. Beginning in 1946, the large-format drip paintings by Jackson Pollock (1912–1956) signified a radical liberation of action painting from traditional notions of composition, with chance and a performative painting process playing a decisive role in the creation of the pictures. In his *Veil Paintings*, whose creation began in 1954, Morris Louis (1912–1962) allowed paint with vivid colour values to flow vertically down the edges of the canvases. He, too, dispensed with the brush and thus with the distinctive individual painter's style, and surrendered an element of control by pouring the paint, but as a representative of Colour Field Painting he focused more on aesthetic effects. Hermann Nitsch (1938–2022), on the other hand, began in 1960 to hurl red paint onto the canvases as 'pourings', in vigorous public acts. These works exist in a completely different context – that of his somewhat cultic 'Orgies Mystery Theatre'. The shock of the Second World War, the liberation and renewal of painting – experienced as an urgent need – the emphatic rejection of figural art occasioned by its political abuse and the desire to break new, experimental ground: all these developments proved formative for these artistic positions. In recent decades, very different artistic values have emerged – for example, in the vertically flowing paintings of Pat Steir (*1940) and John M. Armleder (*1948) or the large-format, painterly environments of Katharina Grosse (*1961). Steir and Armleder's paintings have a conceptual starting point, whereas Grosse's paintings have a constructive or deconstructivist starting point. Ash Keating, on the other

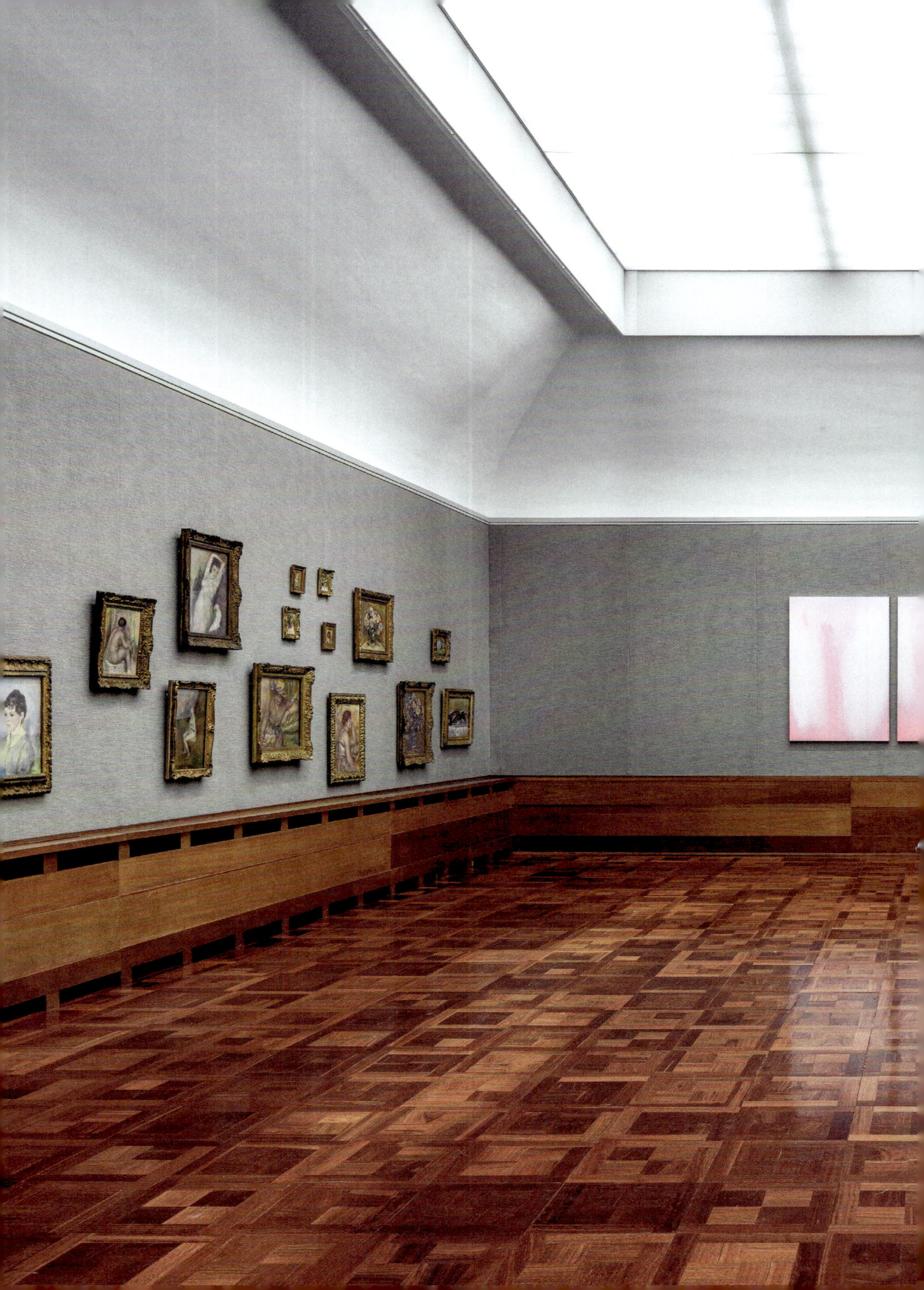

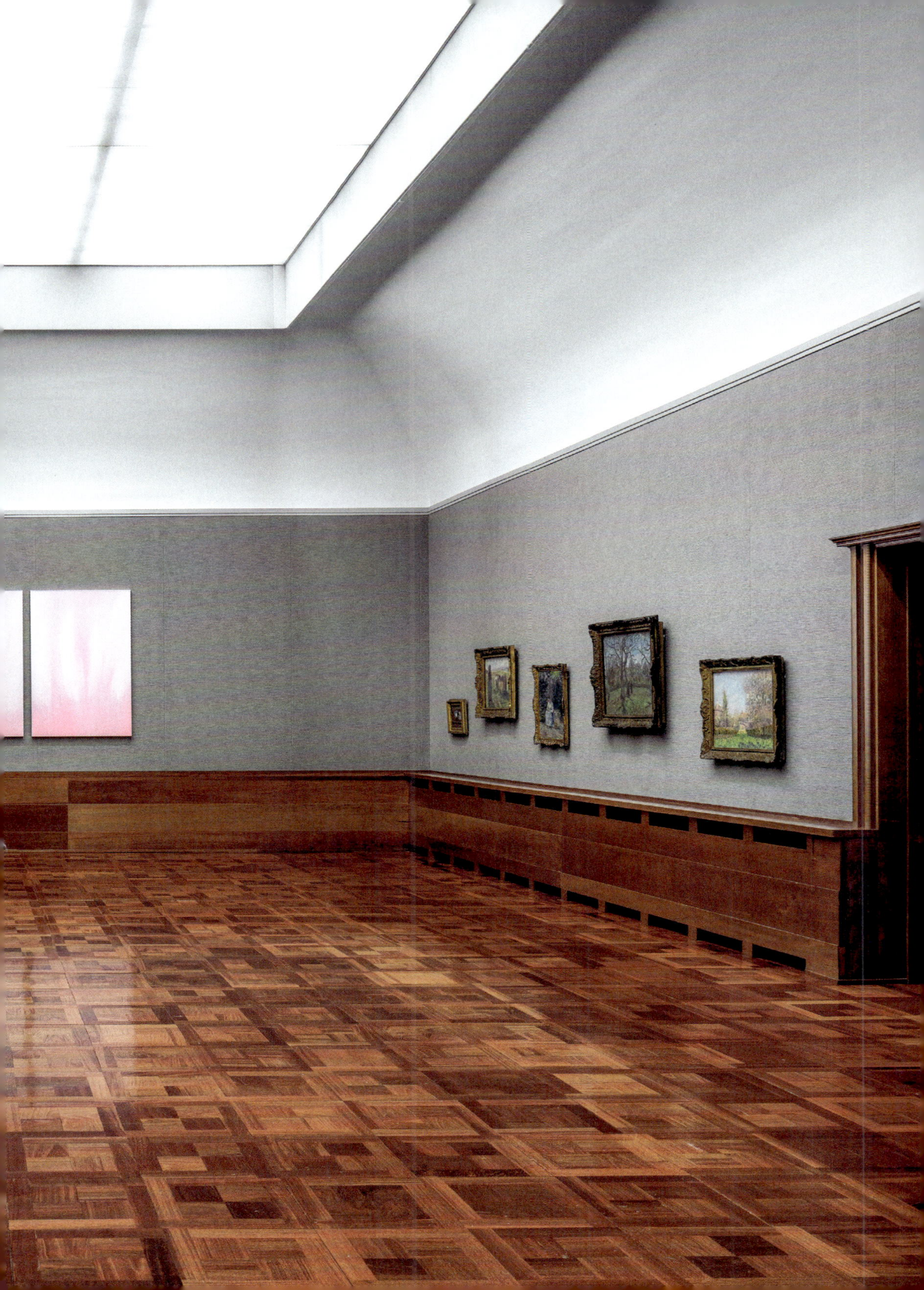

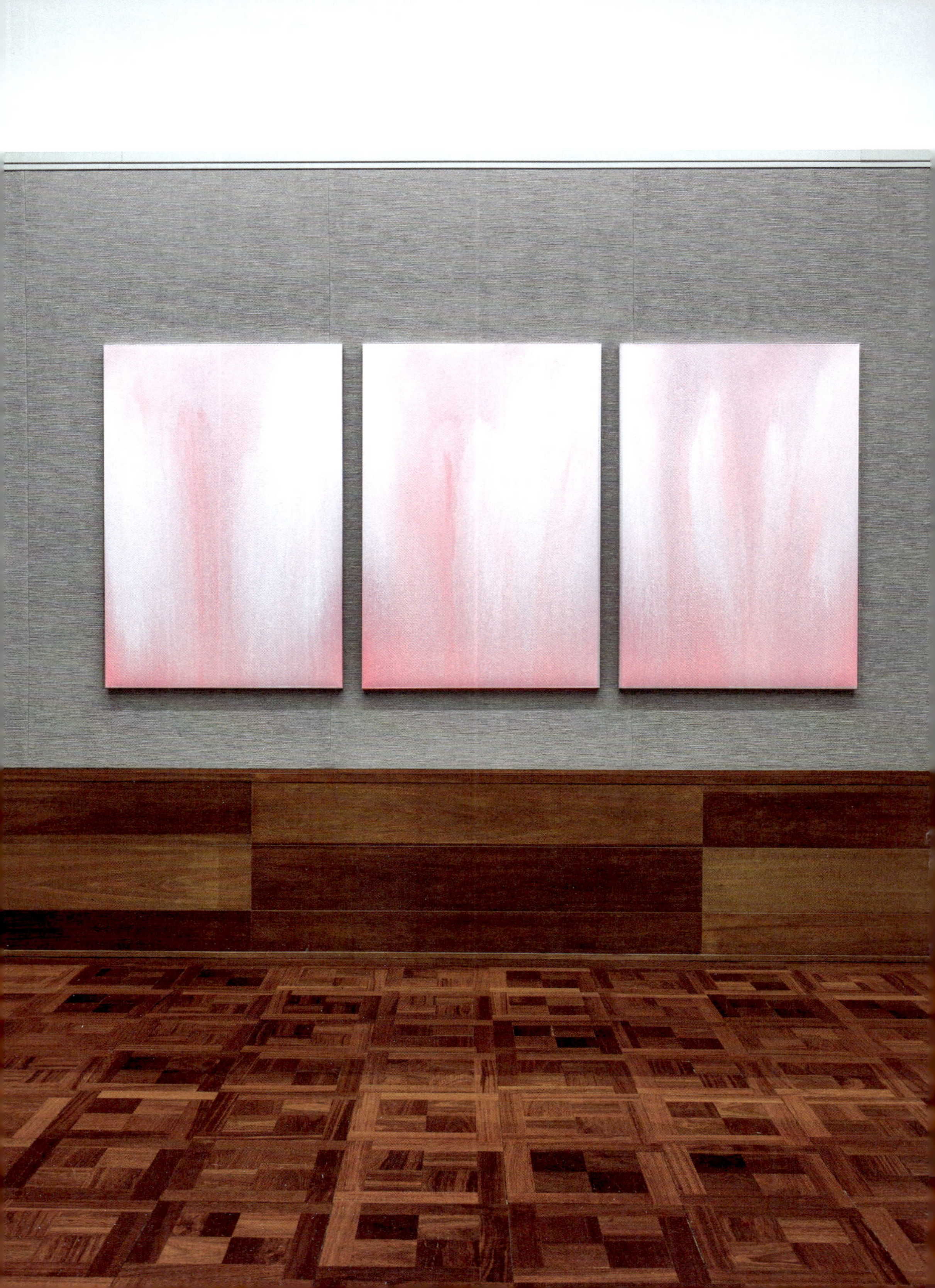

*Gravity System Response, GSR
15_2022 Triptych,* 2022
Acryl auf Leinwand / Acrylic
on linen, je / each 150 x 100 cm

Begegnungen bereits in jungen Jahren mit der immensen Weite und den intensiven Licht- und Farbverhältnissen sind – neben Einflüssen von Hip Hop und Graffiti – seine Ankerpunkte. Die Ausstellung in der Langmatt trägt dem in besonderem Masse Rechnung. *Ice Floes Response* steht beispielhaft für seinen inneren Bezug zum Impressionismus und dessen enger Verbundenheit mit der Natur und ihren sich stets wandelnden Licht- und Farbverhältnissen.

Ausgehend von der Sammlung der rund 50 herausragenden Bilder des französischen Impressionismus legt das Museum Langmatt seit einigen Jahren den Schwerpunkt des Ausstellungsprogramms auf das Medium Malerei. Gegenständliche Positionen (zum Beispiel Rose Wylie, Norbert Bisky) wechseln sich mit ungegenständlichen ab (zum Beispiel Renée Levi, Mark Wallinger). Allen gemeinsam sind mehr oder weniger ausgeprägte Bezüge zum historischen Ensemble Langmatt oder zu den zentralen Eigenschaften des Impressionismus: Licht und Bewegung. Ash Keating erweitert dieses Spektrum durch seine energetische Verwandlung des Verwalterhauses, seine Hommage an Monet und die magische Leuchtkraft von *GSR 15_2022.* Bei allen Kontrasten zum Impressionismus bietet seine Ausstellung eine inspirierende Begegnung der Licht- und Farbwirkungen zweier Epochen.

hand, draws his inspiration from the Australian landscape. His encounters at a young age with that landscape's immense expanse and intense light and colour conditions are – in addition to influences from hip-hop and graffiti – his anchor points. The exhibition in the Langmatt takes this into account to an exceptional degree. *Ice Floes Response* exemplifies his inner connection to Impressionism and its close connection with nature and with the ever-changing light and colour conditions found in nature.

Inspired by its collection of around fifty outstanding French Impressionist paintings, the Museum Langmatt exhibition programme has concentrated on the medium of painting for a number of years now. Representational styles (e. g. Rose Wylie, Norbert Bisky) alternate with non-representational positions (e. g. Renée Levi, Mark Wallinger). What they all have in common is that, to a greater or lesser degree, they connect with the historical Langmatt ensemble or to the key characteristics of Impressionism: light and movement. Ash Keating expands this spectrum through his energetic transformation of the caretaker's house, his homage to Monet, and the magical luminosity of *GSR 15_2022.* Despite all the ways in which it contrasts with Impressionism, his exhibition offers an inspiring encounter between the light and colour effects of two epochs.

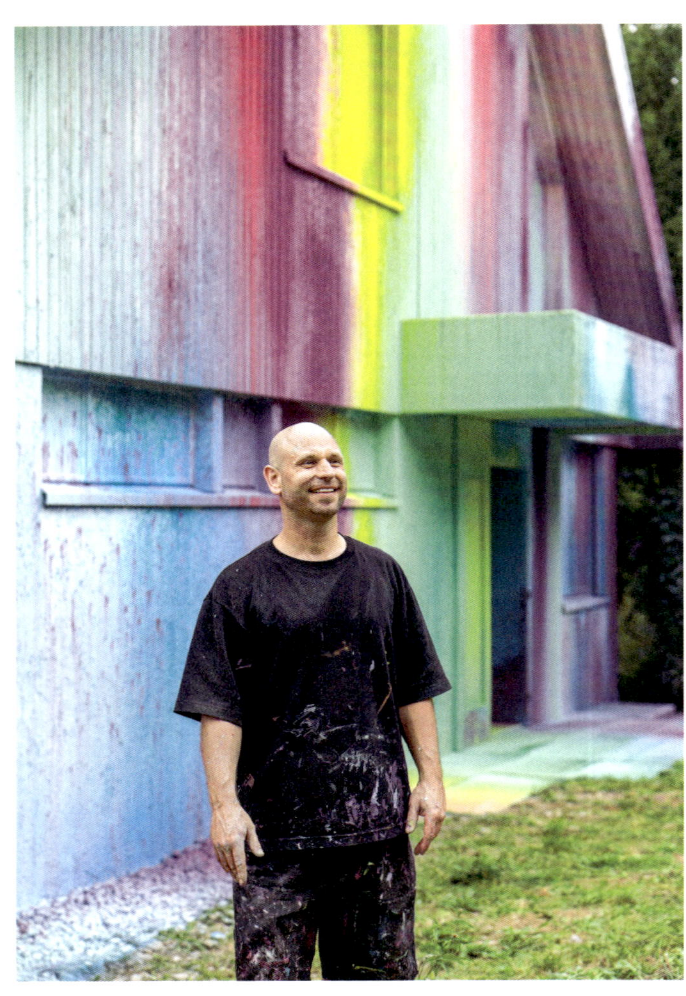

ASH KEATING IM GESPRÄCH MIT MARKUS STEGMANN

Markus Stegmann: How did you become an artist?

Ash Keating: My initial steps were taken at the age of seventeen, with access to art materials at school and the encouragement of art teachers and mentors, to whom I'm still grateful. At the time, my inspiration came from the aerial landscape of Taungurung country in north-east Victoria, which I viewed from the window of my late grandmother's Cessna 150 aeroplane. Throughout the late 1990s, my grandmother and I took turns flying together across this countryside. Being immersed in nature and responding to these experiences with a series of paintings instilled in me the realisation that I ultimately wanted to be an artist. I recently incorporated a similar practice into my painting series *Elevated Horizon Response,* which was inspired by an aerial perspective of similar landscapes to where I had flown years ago.

What was the main influence on you as a young artist?

While I was making my way through art school, in the late 1990s and early 2000s, I was largely unaware of many great artists who had come before me, working in similar ways. Whilst my passion for nature had a profound effect on my work, I was also influenced by hip-hop and graffiti culture. During this time, I was studying full-time during the day and going out at night to experiment with techniques, including manipulating advertising billboards, throwing small pots of free or cheap mis-tinted house paints and puncturing blocked aerosol cans to create gestural abstractions. Even then, my work ethic was strong, as instilled in me by my late mother Pam Keating.

Markus Stegmann: Wie bist du Künstler geworden?

Ash Keating: Meine ersten Schritte in diese Richtung fanden im Alter von 17 Jahren statt, als ich Zugang zu Künstlermaterialien in der Schule hatte, aber auch aufgrund der Ermutigung von Kunstlehrer*innen und Mentor*innen, denen ich immer noch dankbar bin.

Damals stammte meine Inspiration aus Luftansichten der Landschaft von Taungurung Country in North-East Victoria, die ich aus dem Fenster der Cessna 150 meiner inzwischen verstorbenen Grossmutter sah.

Gegen Ende der 1990er-Jahre unternahmen meine Grossmutter und ich gemeinsame Flüge über dieses Land. Dieses Eintauchen in die Natur und die Reaktion auf diese Erfahrungen in Form einer Reihe von Bildern, führten mich zu der Erkenntnis, dass ich im Grunde genommen Künstler sein wollte. Erst kürzlich setzte ich eine vergleichbare Praxis bei meiner Gemäldeserie *Elevated Horizon Response* um, die durch einen Blick aus der Vogelperspektive auf ähnliche Landschaften inspiriert war wie jene, über die ich Jahre zuvor geflogen war.

Was hat dich als junger Künstler hauptsächlich geprägt?

Als ich Ende der 1990er-, Anfang der 2000er-Jahre meinen Weg durch die Kunstschulen machte, war ich mir grösstenteils nicht bewusst, dass viele der grossen Künstler*innen vor mir ähnlich gearbeitet hatten. Obwohl meine Leidenschaft für die Natur tiefgreifenden Einfluss auf meine Arbeiten hatte, war ich auch von Hip-Hop- und Graffiti-Kultur inspiriert.

In dieser Zeit studierte ich tagsüber Vollzeit und ging in der Nacht hinaus, um mit verschiedenen Techniken zu experimentieren; unter anderem manipulierte ich Werbeplakate, warf kleine Töpfe kostenloser oder billiger Fassadenfarbe auf Hauswände und durchstach verstopfte Spraydosen, um gestische Abstraktionen zu schaffen. Schon damals war ich sehr engagiert, was ich meiner verstorbenen Mutter Pam Keating zu verdanken habe.

As access to information increased via the internet, I began to gain exposure to artists like Pat Steir, Hans Hartung and Katharina Grosse. Having experimented with similar techniques and tools of the trade for some time, by this stage my practice had already developed in a distinctive way.

Your works often show a particularly intense colourfulness. Where does that come from?
My use of colour is mostly intuitive, and while the direction is largely drawn from time spent in nature, poster and graphic design make their way into my psyche too.
Seeing how other artists experiment with colour is a constant source of inspiration, but nothing compares to the experience of being in the studio with a wide selection of art materials, spontaneously mixing, diluting and tinting a variety of mediums, and having the ability to freely explore various colour compositions.
In the studio, I love working with iridescent silver as my primary lightener, with or without white tint. For outdoor walls, I typically work with bolder colours on darker backgrounds, which may be due to a sense of nostalgia for one of my earliest large-scale wall paintings in 2002 on a bridge in Canberra, Australia, where I applied gestural marks of ultramarine blue and deep yellow using aerosol cans punctured over black gloss.

Als es über das Internet allmählich immer mehr Zugang zu Informationen gab, begann ich, mich mit Künstler*innen wie Pat Steir, Hans Hartung und Katharina Grosse auseinanderzusetzen. Nachdem ich einige Zeit mit ähnlichen Techniken und Arbeitsinstrumenten experimentiert hatte, entwickelte sich meine Arbeitsweise in eine bestimmte Richtung.

Deine Arbeiten zeigen oft eine besonders intensive Farbigkeit. Woher kommt sie?
Mein Einsatz von Farbe ist in erster Linie intuitiv, und obwohl die Richtung hauptsächlich auf die in der Natur verbrachte Zeit zurückzuführen ist, haben auch Plakat- und Grafikdesign Eingang in meine Arbeit gefunden.
Zu sehen, wie andere Künstler*innen mit Farbe experimentieren, ist eine beständige Quelle der Inspiration, doch nichts lässt sich mit der Erfahrung vergleichen, im Atelier eine grosse Auswahl an Arbeitsmaterialien zur Verfügung zu haben, eine Vielzahl von Medien spontan mischen, verdünnen und färben zu können, und die Möglichkeit zu haben, verschiedene Farbkompositionen ganz frei auszuprobieren.
Im Atelier arbeite ich gerne mit schillerndem Silber als wichtigstem Aufheller, mit oder ohne weisse Tönung. Für Aussenwände wähle ich für gewöhnlich kräftigere Farben auf dunklerem Hintergrund, was vielleicht einem Gefühl der Nostalgie für eines meiner frühesten grossformatigen Wandgemälde entspringt, das 2002 auf einer Brücke in Canberra, Australien, entstanden ist, wo ich gestische Zeichen aus Ultramarin und intensivem Gelb mithilfe von Spraydosen punktuell auf schwarzem Glanzlack aufgetragen habe.

You like to work outside and
paint large buildings or huge walls.
How did this idea come about?
As a teenager, I was painting canvases
in both my high school art department
and in my parents' garage, which required me to move their cars in and out
to accommodate.
With limited space, I yearned for the
freedom to make a mess and create
works on a larger scale, so I began ex-
perimenting on walls and surfaces
in the eastern suburbs of Naarm / Melbourne, often at night when it was
easier to do this without permission.
In my early twenties I began to work on
a larger scale again, painting empty
walls in and around the central busi-
ness district, visiting these places the
next day to view my hurriedly made
creations for the first time, together
with the public.

To paint large areas you are using
fire extinguishers filled with paint.
How did you come up with this idea?
Whilst I certainly can't lay claim to
the idea, I was at the forefront of using
them, both in Melbourne and globally,
in the early 2000s.
After becoming aware that graffiti writ-
ers in Europe were repurposing them
to tag with, I became interested in the
idea of using them to create abstract
wall paintings out of reach of most graffiti. I found a dozen of them in an
abandoned factory and began experi-
menting with making large-scale, lay-
ered paintings by projecting a multi-
tude of coloured paints high up the wall
and adding water to allow the colours
to mix together as they ran down.

Du arbeitest gerne im Aussenraum und
bemalst grosse Gebäude oder riesige
Wände. Wie kam es zu dieser Idee?
Als Teenager malte ich sowohl in der Kunstabtei-
lung meiner High School als auch in der Garage
meiner Eltern, wofür ich ihre Autos immer hinein-
und hinausfahren musste, um Platz zu haben.
Durch diesen ständigen Platzmangel wuchs die
Sehnsucht danach, mich so richtig auszutoben und
grossformatige Arbeiten zu schaffen, also begann
ich, auf Mauern und Oberflächen in den östlichen
Aussenbezirken von Naarm/Melbourne zu experimentieren, oft in der Nacht, wenn es einfacher war,
das ohne Genehmigung zu tun.
In meinen frühen 20ern begann ich, wieder gross-
formatiger zu arbeiten und bemalte leere Wände in
und um das Hauptgeschäftsviertel. Am nächsten
Tag kehrte ich dann dorthin zurück und begutach-
tete meine schnell gemachten Arbeiten zum ersten
Mal, zusammen mit anderen Zuschauer*innen.

Für die grossflächige Bemalung verwendest
du mit Farbe gefüllte Feuerlöscher. Wie bist
du auf diese Idee gekommen?
Ich kann zwar ganz sicher nicht behaupten, dass
die Idee von mir stammt, ich war aber Anfang der
2000er-Jahre einer der ersten, der sie umgesetzt
hat, sowohl in Melbourne als auch weltweit.
Als mir bewusst wurde, dass Graffiti-Künstler*innen in Europa Feuerlöscher umfunktionierten, um
ihre Tags damit zu schreiben, kam mir die Idee, sie
für abstrakte Gemälde an Wänden zu benutzen, die
für die meisten Graffitis ausser Reichweite waren.

Ich fand ein Dutzend davon in einer verlassenen Fabrik und begann zu experimentieren. Ich schuf grossformatige, mehrlagige Bilder, indem ich eine Vielzahl unterschiedlicher Farben hoch an die Wand schleuderte und Wasser hinzufügte, damit sich die Farben beim Herunterrinnen vermischen konnten.

> Wir haben deine Ausstellung in der Langmatt rund eineinhalb Jahre lang vorbereitet und dabei regelmässig per Videocall kommuniziert. Wie war es für dich, die Langmatt erstmals «live» zu erleben? Was waren dabei die besonderen Herausforderungen?

Ich erinnere mich an deine erste E-Mail, als wäre es gestern gewesen.
Durch diese lange Vorbereitungszeit hatten wir die Möglichkeit, sorgfältig zu überlegen, wie wir das Projekt auf andere Bereiche der Langmatt ausweiten könnten, und ich bin besonders froh über die Möglichkeit, ein breites Spektrum meines Schaffens an einem einzigen Ort zeigen zu können. Das umfasst ein experimentelles Triptychon als Reaktion auf das Gemälde von Claude Monet in der Langmatt-Sammlung, die laute und rohe, ortsgebundene Performance-Malerei an Haus Germann und in der Villa das Triptychon *Gravity System Response,* das neben den Impressionisten hängt und in Dialog mit ihnen tritt.

> Als Australier kommst du aus einem anderen kulturellen Umfeld. Wie nimmst du die Langmatt und ihre Geschichte wahr? Was fällt dir besonders auf?

Das Museum Langmatt erinnert mich an das Heide Museum of Modern Art in den östlichen Aussenbezirken von Naarm/Melbourne. Das Land, das ein bedeutender Wurundjeri-Versammlungsort war, den später die australischen Impressionist*innen besuchten, wurde 1934 zum Garten und zur Heimat von John und Sunday Reed. Die Reeds waren

> We prepared your exhibition with Museum Langmatt for about one and a half year's and communicated regularly via video call. How was it for you to experience the Langmatt 'live' for the first time? What were the particular challenges?

I still remember your email like it was yesterday.
Having an extended duration to prepare provided us with the ability to carefully consider how to expand the project across other parts of the Langmatt and I am particularly excited for the opportunity to showcase a diverse range of my practice all in one place. This includes an experimental painting, responding to the Claude Monet painting in Langmatt's collection; the loud and raw site-responsive endurance performance painting on Haus Germann; and within the villa, the *Gravity System Response* studio painting hung alongside and in conversation with the Impressionists.

> As an Australian, you come from a different cultural background. How do you perceive the Langmatt and its history? What do you notice in particular?

Museum Langmatt reminds me of the Heide Museum of Modern Art, in the eastern suburbs of Naarm / Melbourne. Once a significant Wurundjeri gathering place and later visited by artists of the Australian Impressionists, the land became the garden and home of John and Sunday Reed in 1934. The Reeds were friends and patrons of modern artists at the forefront of challenging the entrenched cultural establishment of Australia in the 1940s. Today, there is a new museum on the land, alongside the original house, showcasing the collection the Reed's amassed, alongside contemporary artists working today. So, in some way, this really is a similar story and current format to that of Museum Langmatt.

On 17 August 2023 you completely painted the steward's house. What were the biggest challenges and what was the biggest attraction for you?

While conceptually it may seem simple, significant planning, preparation and the efforts of a number of incredible people were required to make it a success.

I am grateful to Daniela Minneboo for sourcing the initial collection of used, old paints over a period of months, helping to shape my decided colour palette by limiting the selection upon which to incorporate new paints in other shades too.

When I arrived in Baden, my initial inspiration came during time spent in the garden and villa gallery, observing the flowering gardens depicted in several Renoir and Cézanne paintings, as well as the vibrant violets and greens within the gardens of Langmatt.

My aim is always to improvise, letting every mark and action lead to the next. The chosen palette and surrounding garden setting provided the opportunity for something unique.

The key challenges during the creation of the work itself were the progressive, improvised decisions required to build the various compositions to make up the overall shapes of the house.

In the park you are showing a large triptych titled *Ice Floes Response* (2023), an homage to the painting *Ice Floes at Twilight* (1893) by Claude Monet in the Langmatt Collection. What fascinates you about this painting by Monet?

Back in 1893, the notion of ice melting in the painting of Claude Monet had a romantic quality, yet now with greater awareness and severity of the global climate crisis, the concept of ice melting is alarming. It is no coincidence that this summer has been the hottest ever on record across Europe, with fires burning through the Swiss Alps, and Rocky Mountains breaking apart in some areas.

Freunde und Förderer moderner Künstler*innen, die in den 1940er-Jahren an vorderster Front das festgefahrene Kulturestablishment Australiens infrage stellten. Heute befindet sich auf ihrem Land, neben dem ursprünglichen Haus, ein neues Museum, das neben der Sammlung, die die Reeds zusammengetragen haben, auch zeitgenössische Künstler*innen präsentiert. Das ist also gewissermassen eine ähnliche Geschichte wie jene des Museums Langmatt und ein vergleichbares aktuelles Format der Begegnung.

Am 17. August 2023 hast du das Verwalterhaus komplett bemalt. Was waren die grössten Herausforderungen, und was war der grösste Reiz für dich?

Obwohl es konzeptuell einfach wirken mag, erforderte es erhebliche Planung, Vorbereitung und den Einsatz einer Reihe unglaublicher Menschen, um es zum Erfolg zu führen.

Ich bin Daniela Minneboo zu Dank verpflichtet, die über Monate hinweg verschiedene Restposten diverser Farben aufspürte und mir dabei half, mich für eine Farbpalette zu entscheiden, indem die Auswahl an Farben auf diese Weise eingeschränkt war.

Nach meiner Ankunft in Baden kamen die ersten Inspirationen vom Park und der Galerie der Villa, als ich dort blühende Gärten in etlichen Gemälden von Renoir und Cézanne sah, daneben aber auch die leuchtenden Violett- und Grüntöne im Park der Langmatt.

Ich bin stets bestrebt zu improvisieren, jedes Zeichen und jede Handlung zur nächsten führen zu lassen. Die gewählte Farbpalette und die umgebende Parkkulisse boten mir die Gelegenheit für etwas Einzigartiges und Neues.

Die grössten Herausforderungen während der Entstehung der Arbeit selbst waren die andauernden improvisierten Entscheidungen, die nötig waren, um die verschiedenen Kompositionen für die Gesamtform des Hauses zu erschaffen.

Im Park zeigst du das grosse Triptychon *Ice Floes Response* (2023), eine Hommage an das Gemälde *Eisschollen im Dämmerlicht* (1893) von Claude Monet in der Sammlung der Langmatt. Was fasziniert dich an diesem Bild von Monet?

Damals, 1893, hatte die Vorstellung des schmelzenden Eises im Gemälde von Claude Monet noch etwas Romantisches, doch heute, mit dem grösseren Bewusstsein und dem Ernst der weltweiten Klimakrise, ist das schmelzende Eis besorgniserregend. Es ist kein Zufall, dass dieser Sommer der heisseste je verzeichnete Sommer in ganz Europa war, mit Waldbränden in den Schweizer Alpen und Felsstürzen in einigen Gebieten.

Die Installation meines Triptychons als Hommage an *Eisschollen im Dämmerlicht* im üppigen, grünen Park der Langmatt mag zunächst poetisch erscheinen und nicht wie ein Warnsignal vor drohenden Katastrophen. Auf den ersten Blick wirken meine Arbeiten hübsch, bei näherer Betrachtung sind jedoch Zusammenbruch und Verfall erkennbar.

Dieses Gemälde bot die Gelegenheit, mit neuen Techniken zu experimentieren, darunter auch der Einsatz von Handseife als zweiter Schicht und als schablonenartiges Material, ehe ich Berge und Eis über dem Himmel und dessen Spiegelung im Wasser malte. Mithilfe eines Hochdruckwasserschlauches entfernte ich die Seife und arbeitet so die Komposition heraus, wodurch die darunter liegenden, erodierten Teile des Berges hervortraten, die beinahe wie ein Erdrutsch wirken.

Installing my homage to *Ice Floes at Twilight* in the lush green gardens of Langmatt may initially appear to be poetic, rather than a warning sign for any impending disasters we face. At first glance my works are beautiful, yet on closer inspection there is a breakdown and decay taking place. Creating this painting provided an opportunity to experiment with new techniques, including the use of hand soap as a second layer and stencil-like material, before painting the mountains and ice over the top of the sky and its reflection in the water. Applying a high-pressure water hose to remove the soap revealed the deterioration of the mountain beneath, much like a landslide.

Your examination of Monet's painting has meanwhile led to further works. What are you particularly interested in?

After making the larger *Ice Floes Response* paintings, I was interested to further explore the abstraction of the melting ice on a macro level, through a series of textured paintings. After undertaking a rather extensive process, the final result is almost holographic, through the use of interference / pearl colours. As mentioned, the idea of melting ice is very different now and my holographic interpretation is representative of loss and memory. In parallel to the exhibition at Museum Langmatt, I will show these works in Naarm / Melbourne in early September, alongside a similar *Ice Floes Response* painting made at the same time as the works currently displayed in the gardens of Langmatt.

As the third part of your exhibition, we are presenting a triptych from your ongoing series Gravity System Response titled *GSR 15_2022* in the main gallery in dialogue with the highlights of French Impressionism. What are your impressions?
Having my work share the same room as Cézanne, Renoir, Pissarro, Bonnard and Van Gogh is a surreal experience that I am immensely humbled by. The reason I chose this particular triptych for a dialogue with their work is that whilst it commands attention, it does so in a quiet and subtle way. As you enter the villa gallery from a distance, these paintings seem minimal and unassuming. Upon closer inspection, they begin to show their magic, and looking closer again reveal texture and interference pigments that gathered as the water dragged the paint down the surface. The opportunity to engage in a respectful conversation with these great artists was the perfect first time to exhibit this particular painting I created around eighteen months ago.

As an artist you are dependent on exhibition opportunities. What role does Instagram play for you?
Promoting my projects on social media is the most effective way to build awareness of my work internationally. All of my recent international opportunities for exhibitions and painting projects have come from people who follow my art practice on Instagram. As an independent practitioner based in Australia, this is incredibly valuable in enabling me to build my career globally.

Deine Auseinandersetzung mit dem Bild von Monet führte in der Zwischenzeit zu weiteren Werken. Was interessiert dich dabei besonders?
Nach den grösseren *Ice Floes Response*-Bildern wollte ich die Abstraktion des schmelzenden Eises auf Makroebene durch eine Serie reliefartiger Gemälde weiter erkunden. Nach einem recht umfassenden Prozess wirkt das Endergebnis durch den Einsatz von Interferenzfarben beinahe holografisch. Wie bereits erwähnt, ist die Vorstellung von schmelzendem Eis heute eine ganz andere, und meine holografische Interpretation steht für Verlust und Erinnerung.
Parallel zur Ausstellung im Museum Langmatt werde ich diese Arbeiten Anfang September in Naarm/Melbourne zeigen, neben einem ähnlichen *Ice Floes Response*-Gemälde, das zur gleichen Zeit entstanden ist wie das Triptychon, das aktuell im Park der Langmatt zu sehen ist.

Als dritten Teil deiner Ausstellung präsentieren wir das *Triptychon GSR 15_2022* aus deiner Werkserie *Gravity System Response* in der Gemäldegalerie im Dialog mit den Highlights des französischen Impressionismus. Was sind deine Eindrücke?
Dass meine Arbeiten sich einen Raum teilen mit Cézanne, Renoir, Pissarro, Bonnard und Van Gogh ist eine surreale Erfahrung, die mich sehr demütig macht. Ich habe dieses spezielle Triptychon für einen Dialog mit diesen Arbeiten ausgewählt, weil es zwar die Aufmerksamkeit auf sich zieht, dies jedoch auf eine ruhige, subtile Art und Weise. Betritt man die Galerie der Villa, wirken diese Gemälde aus der Entfernung unbedeutend und bescheiden. Bei näherer Betrachtung beginnen sie jedoch, ihren Zauber zu entfalten, und wenn man noch genauer hinsieht, ihre Texturen und Interferenzpigmente zu zeigen, die entstanden, als Farbe und Wasser über die Bildoberfläche gelaufen sind. Die Gelegenheit, in einen respektvollen Dialog mit

In Australia, most of my recent and up-coming exhibition projects have been with institutions, museums and council galleries, based on opportunities that were built up over time. While Instagram plays a part, it is more my overall body of work and in-person conversations that have led to them.
Working hard to accomplish the best outcome I am capable of each time gives me the best chance of being offered further opportunities.

diesen grossen Künstlern zu treten, war der perfekte Moment, um dieses besondere Bild zum ersten Mal zu zeigen, nachdem es vor etwa achtzehn Monaten entstanden ist.

> Als Künstler bist du auf Ausstellungsmöglichkeiten angewiesen. Welche Rolle spielt Instagram für dich?

Meine Projekte in den sozialen Medien zu promoten ist die effektivste Art und Weise, internationale Aufmerksamkeit für meine Arbeiten zu schaffen. Alle aktuellen internationalen Gelegenheiten für Ausstellungen und Kunstprojekte sind von Personen ausgegangen, die mein Kunstschaffen auf Instagram verfolgen. Als unabhängiger Künstler in Australien ist das unglaublich nützlich, um meine Karriere weltweit voranzutreiben.
In Australien finden die meisten meiner aktuellen und kommenden Ausstellungsprojekte in Institutionen, Museen und Städtischen Galerien statt, bei denen sich die Gelegenheiten im Laufe der Zeit ergeben hatten. Obwohl Instagram eine Rolle spielt, sind es hier eher meine Arbeit und die persönlichen Gespräche, die dazu geführt haben.
Ich arbeite hart daran, jedes Mal das bestmögliche Ergebnis zu erzielen, um mir die besten Chancen für eine nächste Gelegenheit zu sichern.

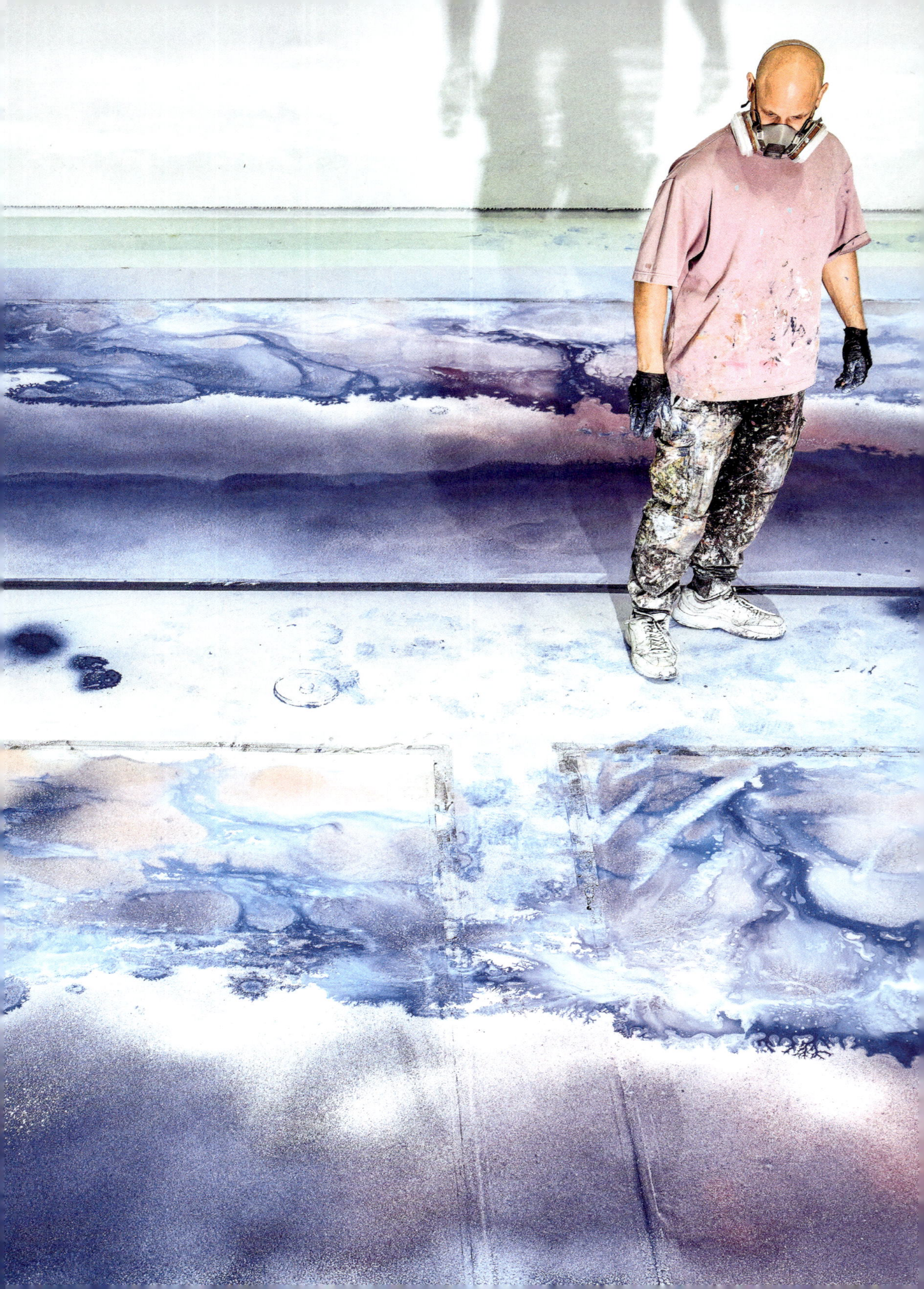

Ash Keating
*1980 in Melbourne, where he still lives today

Ash Keating's artistic work is wide-ranging: it includes site-specific installations, large-scale murals, painting on canvas and performances.
In 2002, he began creating large-format, site-specific works in outdoor spaces.
Since 2004, his work has been shown in numerous exhibitions, and it began appearing internationally in 2006.
The 2023 exhibition at Museum Langmatt is Ash Keating's first solo exhibition in Europe.
Works by Ash Keating are in various public collections, including the National Gallery of Victoria, the National Gallery of Australia, the Museum of Contemporary Art Australia, the Art Gallery of New South Wales, the Monash University Museum of Art and Artbank.

www.ashkeating.com

Ash Keating
*1980 in Melbourne, lebt dort

Die künstlerische Arbeit von Ash Keating weist eine grosse Bandbreite auf: ortsspezifische Installationen, grossformatige Wandmalereien, Malerei auf Leinwand sowie Performances.
Seit 2002 entstehen grossformatige, ortsspezifische Arbeiten im Aussenraum. Seit 2004 wird seine Arbeit in zahlreichen Ausstellungen gezeigt, seit 2006 auch international. Die Ausstellung im Museum Langmatt 2023 ist die erste Einzelausstellung Ash Keatings in Europa.
Werke von Ash Keating sind in verschiedenen öffentlichen Sammlungen vertreten, zum Beispiel National Gallery of Victoria, National Gallery of Australia, Museum of Contemporary Art Australia, Art Gallery of New South Wales, Monash University Museum of Art and Artbank.

Diese Publikation erscheint anlässlich der Ausstellung / This catalogue is published in conjunction with the exhibition

Ash Keating
Museum Langmatt, Baden
20. August – 10. Dezember 2023
20 August – 10 December 2023

Publikation / Publication

Autor*innen / Authors
Ash Keating
Daniela Minneboo
Markus Stegmann

Projektmanagement /
Project management
Richard Viktor Hagemann,
Frauke Berchtig

Lektorat / Copyediting
Frauke Berchtig (Deutsch / German),
Aaron Bogart (Englisch / English)

Übersetzung / Translation
Alison Kirkland (Englisch / English)
Alexandra Titze-Grabec
(Deutsch / German)

Fotonachweis / Photo credits:
Severin Bigler, S./pp. 4/5, 6/7, 8, 13, 18,
19, 21, 36/37, 46/47, 54/55, 56, 60
Ash Keating, S./pp. 20, 22–35, 38/39,
40, 48/49, 51, 58/59, 70

Grafische Gestaltung / Graphic design
Groenlandbasel, Basel

Schriften / Typefaces
ABC Gravity, Monument Grotesk

Reproduktion / Reproductions
Schwabenrepro GmbH

Verlagsherstellung / Production
Kati Klaeske

Papier / Paper
Pergraphica Rough 1.4 Classic, 120 g/m²

Druck und Bindung / Printing and binding
Offizin Scheufele

© 2023 Hatje Cantz Verlag, Berlin,
Museum Langmatt, Baden,
und Autor*innen / and authors

© 2023 für die abgebildeten Werke von /
for the reproduced works by
Ash Keating: der Künstler / the artist

Erschienen im / Published by
Hatje Cantz Verlag GmbH
Mommsenstraße 27, 10629 Berlin
Germany
www.hatjecantz.com
Ein Unternehmen der Ganske
Verlagsgruppe
A Ganske Publishing Group Company

ISBN: 978-3-7757-5516-0
Printed in Germany

Umschlagabbildung / Cover illustration
Haus Germann Response,
Foto / photo: Ash Keating

Ausstellung / Exhibition

Direktor, Kurator / Director, curator
Markus Stegmann

Assistenzkuratorin / Assistant curator
Daniela Minneboo

Administration und
Öffentlichkeitsarbeit /
Administration and public relations
Sabine Fehlmann

Kunstvermittlung / Art education
Vera Horat

Betriebsleitung / Head of operations
Stéphanie Engel, Silla Gröbly,
Susi Stierli

Ausstellungstechnik / Exhibition services
Andreas Rudolf, Fabian Zulliger

Museum Langmatt
Römerstrasse 30, CH-5400 Baden
www.langmatt.ch

Dank / Acknowledgements

Für Betriebsbeiträge danken wir /
We would like to thank for their help with
the operating expenses

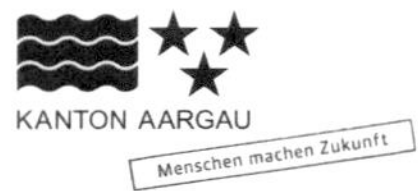

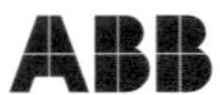

Hauptsponsor / Main sponsor

Co-Sponsor

Für die Unterstützung von Ausstellung
und Publikation danken wir /
We would like to thank the following for
their support of the exhibition and the
publication

Josef + Margrit Killer-Schmidli Stiftung
Freunde Museum Langmatt

Für die Unterstützung der Bemalung
des Verwalterhauses danken wir /
We would like to thank for the support of
the painting of the steward's house

Festgestaltung OK Badenfahrt

Für das Farb-Sponsoring danken wir /
We would like to thank the following for
their sponsoring of colours

Caparol Farben und Lacke, Nänikon
Giuliani AG, Wettingen
RUCO LACKE & FARBEN, Glattbrugg/
Baden